A PLANETARY AV

CU00810588

COMMENTS BY REVIEWERS:

"From my perspective as a life-long s ....,
I think Kathy Newburn provides a clear and easily understandable ex-
position of the often complicated and complex wisdom that has been
given to humanity in the form of what the Tibetan Teacher Himself has
termed the 'intermediate' teachings of the Ageless Wisdom—the first
'preparatory' teachings having been given out in the two tomes brought
forth by Helena Petrovna Blavatsky in the late 1800s under the titles of
Isis Unveiled and *The Secret Doctrine.* In *A Planetary Awakening* Kathy
Newburn provides a significant glimpse into the forces and energies that
underlie the happenings of the times. She easily accomplishes her goal
of providing the interested reader with 'a deeper understanding of what
is occurring in the world today,' while providing an opportunity for the
reader to mindfully and consciously participate in the global consciousness shift at this time of the dawning Age of Aquarius."

Ida Urso, Ph.D., Founder/President, Aquarian Age Community

"Newburn's remarkable presentation on the Bailey books makes
these teachings easily approachable. Her deep knowledge of esotericism
and her ability to structure the presentation cogently give this volume
its unique clarity. It's a must-read for anyone looking to become familiar
with esoteric teachings."

Andrew Binstock

"This book is for the 'new generation' of traveler as well as the experienced one. We all need a guide on our spiritual journey at one time or
another. Kathy Newburn is that guide in *The Planetary Awakening...*"

Rose Cirigliano, playwright, "Where Do I Go From Agropoli?"

"At last, a much-needed, much-awaited book incorporating the
Ageless Wisdom philosophy with practical guidance and solutions to
the difficult problems of our own time. Our seemingly chaotic world
has meaning and purpose beyond our wildest imagining, and this book
explains what we need to know and to do in order to align our thoughts
and actions to create a new world civilization based on right relationship
with all life."

Barbara Anniballi

"*A Planetary Awakening* is a book for the new millennium. It offers clarification and understanding of the present crises facing humanity and our planet and the opportunities these provide to those who seek a closer relationship with the soul and what lies beyond. In a readable, conversational style, Kathy Newburn skillfully presents the timeless insights of the Ancient Wisdom teachings and the way by which we can fulfill our destiny of serving the underlying purpose and plan for humanity. This book is essential reading for all those who strive to respond to the note of truth within the heart and mind and to expand the consciousness by reaching out towards a higher reality."

Belinda Baird, teacher, Wellington, New Zealand

"*A Planetary Awakening* is a book whose time has come. It contains a wealth of information that addresses how we can create the changes that need to occur before we—humanity—can move forward into greater light. Written by Kathy Newburn, who has deep insight into problems of our time, it answers many questions and provides a guide to creating a new, much-needed paradigm."

Iris Spellings, Fine art photographer

"This is a much needed book as it clearly explains who we are and what our destiny is. A golden destiny, in truth, once we are able to unveil the clouds surrounding us and look face-to-face at our true Self."

Joaquin Tamames, investment banker, Madrid, Spain

"I have known Kathy Newburn for over twenty years. We have worked together as part of a group both on physical plane projects and on more subjective levels. Our main purpose has always been to help think through and anchor the ideas so essential for humanity as a whole to choose a sane path into the future. These ideas concern the spiritual responsibilities of humanity—the need to cultivate goodwill, the need to care for our planet the earth, the need to replace selfishness with altruism, and finally the challenge to understand and help unfold the spiritual destiny of humanity.

"Kathy's initiative in writing this book is a part of this process. I am sure that its value will be recognized and that it will fulfill its role in awakening more people to the urgency and opportunity of our present time."

Simon Marlow, pianist, England

A PLANETARY AWAKENING

REFLECTIONS ON THE TEACHINGS OF THE TIBETAN IN THE WORKS OF ALICE A. BAILEY

Kathy Newburn

BLUE DOLPHIN PUBLISHING

Published by Blue Dolphin Publishing, Inc.
P.O. Box 8, Nevada City, CA 95959
Orders: 1-800-643-0765
Web: www.bluedolphinpublishing.com

ISBN: 978-1-57733-217-6

Cover art by Amena Divine

Library of Congress Cataloging-in-Publication Data

Newburn, Kathy.
    A planetary awakening : reflections on the teachings of the Tibetan
in the works of Alice A. Bailey / Kathy Newburn.
        p. cm.
    Includes bibliographical references.
    ISBN 978-1-57733-217-6 (pbk. : alk. paper)
    1. Spirituality—Miscellanea. 2. Spiritual life—Miscellanea.
3. Occultism. 4. Djwhal Khul. 5. Bailey, Alice, 1880-1949.
I. Bailey, Alice A. II. Title.

    BF1999.N45 2007
    299'.93—dc22
                                                            2007010513

The Alice Bailey books are quoted with the permission of
Lucis Trust, which holds copyright.

Printed in the United States of America

10   9   8   7   6   5   4   3   2   1

for a new generation of seekers

Signs from the soul come silently
as the sun enters an awakening world.

Tibetan proverb

CONTENTS

FOREWORD

If we had to sum up in a single word the essence within the entire body of teaching of the ages, called forth by the greatest human need, it would have to be: Awareness. All of our Earth-career refinement, distilled from both education and experience, is drawn by the demand to elevate the quality, and keep expanding the field, of our self-conscious awareness. There is no part of our being that can be excluded from participating in what is destined to give this crown of all our endeavors, its very shape and definition.

What we actually perceive, when we look out to make sense of our world, is very closely tied up with what we bring to it. In truth, what we see is determined by how we are able to look at it. Needless to say, this inevitably conditions the nature of our reactions, which in turn greatly influence, even determine, the quality of our lives. The grades that mark the progress reached on the evolutionary scale of our awareness are not only the stepping stones of our realization, but the elements of meaning in the interpretation of our reality. As within, so without.

Because we are far more conscious of our individual needs than the many cries that surround us, we are not entirely aware that the larger world we are a part of, is also a part of us. How really conscious are we of the fact that what upholds and sustains us also needs us? Because we belong to each other, the needs of one are inseparably fused with the needs of the other.

Here is one area to remind us that this progressively more elevated consciousness must ever be reached for: To lead us to the mature vision that is capable of rising above the smallness of one's self in order to be able to see others in a better light. To bring us back from the extreme of judgment to the center of balance and compassion, where our old values transform, to uphold and blend with our higher motivated priorities. Only with our own transformation from within, can we become a living, integral part of the larger universal effort, now striving to make our planet better, safer and a more enlightened place.

A Planetary Awakening was written as a contribution to this endeavor and is presented as a labor of love to both established workers and the new generation of seekers.

The effects of a coming new era with its grand sweeping energies are already being felt in our lives and continue to bring along major changes, but these events in no way diminish the sovereignty of our free will, nor do anything at all to relieve us from the burden of its responsibility. To make real progress on the path of life, both in the sense of the mundane and the spiritual, we are required by the Law that governs all Life, to make outstanding, intelligent and responsible choices, not just some of the time or when we feel like it, but always. With all the efforts we are capable of, we must come forward to offer what is the best within us and make it available in service for the uplifting of all humanity and the planet for our common, brighter tomorrow. The tireless aspiration to keep reaching for what is better and higher, both within us and on the way toward our shared goal, is the living thread of light that links us not only with each other but also with our higher center, where our unity is far more real than the appearance of our temporary separation.

A great Indian teacher when asked by disciples to elaborate on the Vedas, replied: "You'll find the significance of the four books within these four words: Be good, do good."

None of the teachings of the world's treasured writings are made available to take students away from the practical plane of life, but rather to bring them back. A spiritually inspired life is the living example of scriptural truth, which does not miss a single opportunity in service to heal, uplift and enlighten. It does not miss a chance to comfort and encourage all those who may have been lagging on the road, under the weight of their heavy burden. A life inspired by the teachings will also remind us that in spite of the difficulties, it's a joy to share the human condition if we strive toward the realization, that only in the fire of our trials are our weaknesses burned out. As we bond in service and grow together in consciousness, our unity in the greater purpose of the Divine Plan will stand revealed.

Joseph Balint
New York
March 2007

INTRODUCTION

Faith is the bird that feels the light and sings when the dawn is still dark.

Rabindranath Tagore

Behind all the harshness and suffering in our world there exists a quiet stirring within the human heart that provides the seed for the profound changes on the horizon. All around us and within us, on the most fundamental level, something far deeper than we have ever known or experienced is attempting to come to birth. As we begin to awaken to what is occurring, our direction changes and we find ourselves following a new way, a new path. We begin to take our cues from an inner compass and no longer from the many strident voices that too often seek to pull us in a myriad of directions. We move in concert with the gentle voice that penetrates our consciousness at odd moments—leaving impressions, fleeting indications, of a majesty that we can't fully capture, let alone comprehend.

Sometimes, because of its very fragility, this voice fails to penetrate into the coarseness of our daily lives. Too often the outer things, with their immediacy and fleeting pleasures, command our attention in ways that leave us encased within the walls of ourselves and the veils of this world—forgetting our true "master." A call if not responded to, a knock if ignored, causes the doors of inner perception to close, at least for a time. So, in order to travel this way, we are asked to pay attention and awaken to the opportunities that are seeking to reveal themselves.

All that we find so beautiful in this world of ours—its people and the love that we can share, the subtleties of nature, the delicacies of fine art and the power of music—pales in comparison with the beauty that exists within. Many people today understand this and are cultivating and nurturing a deep well of silence within themselves, a well that sustains them amidst the surface fragmentation. These moments, the interludes, provide the seeds that will come to fruition at another, gentler time. We are laying this foundation now, both within ourselves and within the world at large, for a flowering of consciousness and spirit that will be greater, vaster and nobler than anything we have ever known.

* * * * *

Much of the material in this book is adapted from the writings of Alice Bailey. Her work spanned twenty-four volumes, nineteen of which were written in cooperation with Djwhal Khul, a Tibetan teacher, between the years 1919 and 1949. She served as an amanuensis through whom "the Tibetan's" ideas were filtered and put into written form. And although there was no physical contact between them during their thirty-year association, their minds became increasingly attuned to each other through the work that they undertook.

Because a large part of the information contained within the Bailey books is not amenable to verification, a determination as to its truth or falsity is left up to the reader. As the Tibetan wrote of himself and his work,

> Suffice it to say, that I am a Tibetan disciple of a certain degree, and this tells you but little, for all are disciples from the humblest aspirant up to, and beyond, the Christ Himself. I live in a physical body like other men, on the borders of Tibet, and at times (from the exoteric stand point) preside over a large group of Tibetan lamas, when my other duties permit....

I am a brother of yours, who has traveled a little longer upon the Path than has the average student, and has therefore incurred greater responsibilities. I am one who has wrestled and fought his way into a greater measure of light than has the aspirant who will read this article, and I must therefore act as a transmitter of the light, no matter what the cost.

The books that I have written are sent out with no claim for their acceptance. They may, or may not, be correct, true and useful. It is for you to ascertain their truth by right practice and by the exercise of the intuition.[2]

The Tibetan and Alice Bailey understood fully that the ideas contained within these teachings were merely one part of a continually unfolding revelation of spiritual truth. They asked their readers to keep this in mind constantly so as to prevent the crystallization of the work into yet one more dogmatic sectarian cult. Alice Bailey frequently asserted that the teaching she was aiding in producing contained merely the ABCs of the Tibetan's knowledge and that she would gladly abandon it in the future if she came upon a deeper manifestation of truth.

The Tibetan had many different responsibilities, including those of a high lama. He is part of an unseen band of enlightened beings of compassion and wisdom who work behind the scenes to guide and protect humanity. They have been known by various names in the different wisdom traditions of the world, including the White Brotherhood, the Spiritual Hierarchy, the Society of Organized Minds and the Masters of the Wisdom. The Tibetan is said to be one of the most learned of all the teachers and it is part of his responsibility to bring forth this wisdom wherever he finds a response.

The ideas and concepts that comprise the Bailey books, therefore, emanate from a level of consciousness that transcends that of an ordinary individual. The teaching forms part of a body of work that has come to be known as the Ageless Wisdom, ancient principles that have been passed down through the ages and kept alive in oral, written, and symbolic form. While this teaching is old, it possesses a nature and depth that can meet the needs of each new generation of seekers.

The bulk of this book is an attempt to present a small portion of that material as it relates specifically to the present crises and opportunities unfolding upon our planet. The value of this teaching lies in the fact that it helps us to understand the subjective factors underlying these outer events as well as providing a systematic method of spiritual training that is safe and has stood the test of time. This is an important consideration because safeguards are essential on the path of spiritual development as we are brought into contact with fiery energies that can wreak havoc in our lives if precautions are not undertaken. Caution and discrimination are necessary in the present spiritual marketplace.

This book could, perhaps, best be described as a reflection on the original writings in the light of the changing conditions in the world today. It includes a distillation of my understanding that has evolved over the course of many years of study and life experience. Hopefully the inclusion of my personal views will not distort the fundamental points of the Ageless Wisdom teachings that have inspired them. I have attempted to present these ideas in a style and language that might serve the needs of a new generation who can, in turn, bring this message to the world. Perhaps one of the reasons why the young have not demonstrated much interest in the Ageless Wisdom teachings is because we have not understood the importance of adapting our message to a form they would find appealing. This book only touches the surface of ideas contained within the original writings and it is my sincere hope that the reader will be encouraged to study them. I have attempted, wherever possible, to reference the original text and any omissions upon my part are by no means an attempt to "claim" the teaching as my own.

This teaching contains ideas that many people will consider outside the realm of possibility and they will reject them out of hand. Others will question why we should consider things that we cannot prove. But there are also others whose minds and hearts are seeking a deeper understanding of what is occurring in the world today. This book is for them.

CHAPTER 1

A TIME OF TRANSITION

> There has never been a period in our planetary history in which opportunity has loomed so large or when so much spiritual light and force could be contacted and utilised by humanity.
>
> Alice Bailey, *Discipleship in the New Age, Vol. II*

THE AQUARIAN AGE

A recent post in an online chat room by physicist Stephen Hawking asked, "In a world that is in chaos politically, socially and environmentally, how can the human race survive the next hundred years?" In a matter of days twenty-five thousand responses poured in—stirring up an internet storm—offering all kinds of suggestions as to how to resolve our planetary problems. Some people (including Hawking himself) suggested we move to another planet while others called upon God or technology to save us. Some questioned if there was ever a time when the world was not in chaos politically, socially and environmentally. Hawking's favorite response came from "Semi-Mad Scientist" who wrote, "Without the belief that we will continue to grow and overcome the pains of social chaos as we mature as a species, we might as well not have any faith at all. I'm not talking religion ... but simply the ... belief that we will survive just as much as the sun will rise the next day."

As we witness the events unfolding on our planet, we know that our future hangs in the balance. It is a time of crisis and change, when everything is being brought to the surface, and the result is at once appalling and fantastic. According to the Ageless Wisdom teaching the stage is being set for us to move into the most important period in the entire history of life on Earth. What is unfolding is, in fact, a spiritual revolution that is broader than any ideology or religious movement. It is not fueled by dogma, but rather by deep changes that are occurring within the very fabric of consciousness itself. But, as with all revolutions, the present one is being born out of the pain, anguish and destruction of the times—for these are the birth pangs of a new world.

The death of old and outmoded ways of living and being ever precedes the incoming of something new. On some level people understand and sense that we are entering the time long foretold in the Scriptures and prophetic writings of the world, when great and momentous events are due to unfold and hidden mysteries will be revealed. But humanity has failed repeatedly to learn the lessons of the past and has succumbed to selfishness and material-ism, which has caused delays in the process. We have not heeded the warnings of the scientists, futurists, historians, economists and spiritual leaders who have been attempting to call for a change in direction. It is probable, therefore, that the present crises will only increase in the years ahead, but so will the light of the new day that is so close at hand. The Ageless Wisdom teachings provide us with information and spiritual tools that can help us stand steady amidst the difficulties and harness our spiritual power to help turn this situation around.

Anyone who is familiar with the popular culture of the six-ties will have heard about the dawning of the Age of Aquarius. That idea, however, wasn't merely fodder for a good pop song or the invention of flower children—it reflects an actual process, an astronomical event that has been underway for several hundred years. Every two thousand to twenty-five hundred years the en-ergy conditioning our planet changes as our sun moves into a new zodiacal influence or constellation. This movement into a new age can be verified astronomically, as well as, astrologically. At the present time we are moving out of the Piscean Age and entering into the Age of Aquarius.[3]

During such times there is always a period of several hundred years when the energies of the old, outgoing constellation overlap and blend with those of the new and incoming influences and neither is fully controlling. It is often a nebulous and confusing time as both the progressive and conservative elements within society seek dominance. The old and outworn ways of living and being that may have been suitable to the earlier time and generation must be cleared away as they no longer meet humanity's needs and clash with the new time and generation that are coming in.

The Piscean Age saw humanity develop many positive qualities that were demonstrated most notably as a heightened sensitivity and a deep yearning for spiritual truth that manifested through the world's religions and within the field of education and higher learning. Collectively we made great strides in our understanding of the natural world, especially through the discoveries of science that have done so much to improve our lives and to expand our consciousness. The focus of the Piscean Age was upon obedience to external authority and devotion and reverence toward God.[4]

Under the influence of the energies of Aquarius, the focus is shifting from religion to a broad-based spirituality and to recognition of the authority of the soul, the master within. As these energies come into increasing dominance, the barriers and isolation that are so characteristic of contemporary life will break down. Brotherhood will be the keynote of the age—a brotherhood that is an outer expression of the essential interconnectedness of all life.

Aquarius is the champion of freedom, and we can begin to see the awakening of this influence throughout the world today as large groups of people who were previously oppressed or powerless are finding a voice, possibly for the first time. Each passing decade brings a fuller tide of this influence into our midst. This is causing the power base of the planet to shift as people come to recognize they can effect change. Over the past few decades we have allowed those individuals who possess a retrogressive mindset to set the tone of our civilization with the consequences that we witness everywhere today. Part of the present momentum is an attempt to move beyond stopgap measures and shortsighted attempts to patch up forms that have essentially outlived their usefulness, to a re-examination of the entire set of assumptions that underlie our institutions and our very way of life.

This re-examination must extend to include our inner life as well as we come to understand that our spiritual practice has a larger, more universal purpose beyond our own development. Spiritual impression has been interrupted on our planet, creating interference within the divine circulatory flow of energy. It is the task of all seekers to restore this flow and stop this interference.[5]

The day of opportunity is upon us, but it will not last forever. It is time, therefore, for those with a broad humanitarian world-view, who sense the importance of the times, to take back the reins of our planet and thereby ensure justice and well-being for all. Only through human participation, in a spirit of cooperation and goodwill, can we bring this new world into being. In this way, the forward-looking people will move from being a disparate and loosely affiliated group into a potent, living organism—an organism through which powerful spiritual energies can flow, bringing light to all humanity and, indeed, to all life forms.

The Sufis say that when you begin to take your spiritual life seriously you polish the mirror of the heart. When this polishing occurs simultaneously among many people—across national, generational, racial and ethnic lines—it provides the seed of an awakening that unites us at the fundamental level of the spirit and defies the separateness and selfishness of the times. This is happening now.

THE EARTH: A LIVING ORGANISM

> All is related.
>
> Niklas Nihlen

Many people today have come to recognize the Earth as a living Being, the embodiment of a great Life. In the wisdom teachings this Life is known by such names as Sanat Kumara, the Lord of the World, the Ancient of Days, the Eternal Youth. He has chosen to watch over the evolution of humanity until each "weary pilgrim has found his way home" and because of this he is also known as "the Great Sacrifice." Within this great Life we "live and move and have our being." The concerns of many people today are turning towards the need to care for this Life and protect it from continued abuse and possible destruction. All life needs nurturing, but for too long humanity has ignored its responsibility and has wantonly taken and polluted the planet, resulting in the present crisis and imbalance.

Like us, this great Being passes through different stages in its path of evolutionary development. According to the Ageless Wisdom teachings, at the present time this Life is undergoing a major transformation in consciousness, a cosmic initiation that is having a ripple effect upon all forms of life and all kingdoms in nature,[6] but particularly the human. This initiatory process is bringing into outer manifestation certain qualities and creative capacities that have long been dormant and hold much promise for the future. The initiatory periods in the life experience of the Logos are naturally of tremendously long duration, unfolding over aeons of time, but we come to understand that the present period is a great culminating one that will result in a tremendous expansion of all forms of life that are held within the aura of this great Being.

Many people understand that within the planet, just as within the human being, there are centers, sometimes called chakras. These are the points or "nadis" for the distribution of energy. The present stimulation has caused a quickening or vivification within these centers, and a rare, temporary alignment has been established that is potent and far-reaching in its implications. The three major centers within the planet are Shamballa (the center of divine Will), Hierarchy (the center of divine love), and Humanity (the center of creative intelligence).

SHAMBALLA

Shamballa is the highest and most powerful spiritual center, the "center where the Will of God is known." In the ancient books of the East, as well as in myth and legend, it is sometimes known as *Shangri-la*. Christ called it the Father's House, and it was that force that He contacted for the first time in the Garden of Gethsemane.[7] Shamballa is said to be the only place of perfect peace upon the planet; it is the custodian of the "peaceful, silent will."

Shamballa doesn't exist upon the physical plane; it exists within etheric substance,[8] the vital energy body that substands, or underlies, the physical form, creating synthesis and bringing all forms together "within the circle of divine love."[9] Sanat Kumara, the Great Lord, resides in Shamballa and all forms of life are held within the radiance of his aura. The Shamballa force cuts away at the artificial distinctions that divide by race, sex, religion and nationality, and unites us at the fundamental level of our common humanity and spiritual heritage.

Energy is impersonal and stimulates both the good and bad, depending upon the level of consciousness. The energy of Shamballa destroys all that hinders the free expression of the spiritual impulse that is coming to birth at this time. But it is essential that humanity come to a deeper understanding of how to harness and use this energy as a means of effecting real change within the planet. Sometimes certain types of spiritually inclined people have great difficulty in entertaining the possibility of using spiritual energy to bring about the destruction of inhibiting, negative forces. But it is precisely this focused ability that is needed today.

This Shamballa energy is exceedingly powerful and we are unaccustomed to it. This is one of the reasons why life is so challenging at this time and why so many people experience difficulty maintaining emotional and mental equilibrium; their brain cells are receiving too much stimulation. Prior to the last century, energy from Shamballa only impacted directly upon human consciousness twice within the long history of life on this planet. But in recent years there have been three impacts from Shamballa—during World War Two,[10] then in 1975, and finally in 2000. The Shamballa impact at the close of the war was a defining moment in planetary history, not only upon the battlefield but also within the realm of consciousness. It was unclear a few years earlier whether or not humanity would be able to take right action and summon up the will to combat Fascism. As a result of the triumph of the Allied forces, in June of 1945 humanity successfully passed through a moment of crisis and achieved a temporary state of unification and alignment within consciousness that led to the opening of the door of opportunity. The World Teacher reached his "point of decision"—the decision to return to visible presence on Earth as soon as possible and considerably earlier than had been planned prior to that time.[11] The two subsequent impacts from Shamballa in 1975 and again in 2000 have served to continue the preparatory work for this great event by raising the vibratory rate within humanity. The ramifications of these more recent impacts are still working out at this time.

HUMANITY: THE FORERUNNERS

In many respects, humanity is the key point or center within the planet at this time. The destiny of all life on our planet depends upon the decisions we take within the next few years. Many men and women throughout the world are responding to this sense of urgency and are ushering in new ways of living and working, laying the foundation for the Aquarian Age. And just as in the past the world was led by strong and dominant individuals, the future world will be led by strong and effective groups.

The new groups and their members are not necessarily organized and outwardly recognized. They are not concerned with numerical strength or personal authority. They will not seek to put forward their own agenda or dogma or step forth as leaders and teachers. Instead, they seek to understand each other and their different paths and traditions. They work cooperatively, because they understand the strength that flows through a united effort. They are preparing human consciousness for the spiritual events that are due to unfold within the coming decades.[12]

The situation is, of course, fluid and dependent upon human free will. Only a few people at this time grasp the vision of the future and sense the beauty of the emerging Plan, but it is they, in their united striving, who carry a potency and strength that far outweighs their numbers. There are many others, working in all the many departments of human living, who while unaware of the spiritual underpinnings of the present situation, nonetheless are working to meet human and planetary needs as they understand them. These forward-looking individuals and groups are the forerunners of the new age, analogous to St. John the Baptist, who paved the way two thousand years ago for the Christ who emerged at the dawning of the Piscean Age. This group is attempting to alert a seemingly deaf humanity to the auspicious nature of the times.

THE EMERGING AVATARS

Whenever there is a withering of the law and an uprising of lawlessness on all sides, *then* I manifest Myself.

For the salvation of the righteous and the destruction of such as do evil, for the firm establishing of the Law, I come to birth age after age.

The Bhagavad Gita, Book IV, Sutra 7, 8

According to the wisdom tradition a number of teachers, sometimes called Avatars, are now preparing to return to outer manifestation. These Avatars have been defined as extraordinary teachers who from time to time appear to change the face of the world.[13] During periods of difficulty and apparent darkness, when humanity has lost its way, great teachers have come forward to lead us into the light. They help to ease suffering and restore a sense of order and balance in the world. They work to bring to an end the old and undesirable ways of living and being and to make way for the new forms that will more adequately house the incoming light. They come in times of excess and apparent darkness—when the problems confronting us seem beyond our capacity to adequately resolve. And for this reason, if for no other, such teachers may be looked for at this time.

It is unlikely, however, that the coming teachers will step forward under the guise of any one particular religion, as this would only limit the effectiveness of the work they come to undertake. We live in a largely secular world in which many people no longer adhere to established faiths, and the presentation of these teachers as religious figures would leave many people out. The wisdom teachings are attempting to convey a new and broader interpretation of these concepts, one that moves beyond religion and into the more inclusive realm of spirituality. What we are preparing for is a planetary awakening of such magnitude that it will transcend—at the same time that it includes—all the world's faiths.

The problem is that we have as yet little understanding of how contemporary spiritual teachers would look and act. They will have to meet the needs of people today and not be throwbacks to another time. More often than not we tend to imagine them through the lens of the historical Jesus. The picture of a sorrowful and submissively sweet-natured individual, however, is said to have little resemblance to the facts.[14] The coming teachers have much more accurately been described as "supreme spiritual executives," men and women of extraordinary capacities who will be able to implement sweeping changes in the direction of our planetary civilization.

These teachers are different from the way they have been presented by many of the spiritual and religious groups active in the world at this time. They do not head these groups or run any of the outer, physical-plane ashrams, spiritual communities or esoteric organizations that are so widespread today. Within the lineages of the different religious and/or spiritual traditions the world has been blessed with the grace of countless teachers such as Lahiri Mahasaya, Sri Yukteswar, Paramahansa Yogananda, Ramana Maharshi, Sri Ramakrishna, Swami Vivekanada, Master Nan, the many Tibetan teachers and many, many others who worked to bring forward spiritual truths. These teachers have done so much to prepare the way and they stand within the ranks of the Hierarchy but the coming teachers will not necessarily present themselves as gurus and sages as we live in a different time. They will come forward as contemporary individuals, seemingly ordinary, who will however be exceedingly accomplished and powerful in the work that they do.

The coming teachers form an integral part of humanity itself, and under the Law of Rebirth they have transcended our present limitations and emerged into a condition of liberation. They have all passed through the human stage of development. As a result, they know full well the difficulties and triumphs, the joys and sorrows of the human experience in its many dimensions. Their point of departure lies in the realm of consciousness. Through their own efforts they were able to achieve a release from the confines of life that we experience and consequently have attained a greatly enhanced ability to serve. They form part of what is known as the spiritual Hierarchy of our planet, the fifth kingdom, the kingdom of souls.

At the present time they live quietly behind the scenes, unrecognized and unknown, in different nations, scattered throughout the magnetized areas of the world that provide them with the right conditions for their subjective work. Each one of them stands as a focal point for the distribution for the energy of love and wisdom.[15] Quite a number of them have lived in and around the borders of Tibet and northern India—within the protection and sanctity provided by those sacred lands. The Chinese invasion and rape of the "land of the snows" has, however, surely forced them to relocate to more remote areas within the Himalayan range.

As they emerge from their retreats, they will make no claims or call themselves Masters or the like. In some cases they may pass unnoticed, but they will be respected and recognized for the vast and sweeping changes they set in motion. It is the "false prophets" and the fanatics of all faiths and spiritual traditions (who are so widespread at this time) who proclaim the greatness of their lives and work, malign the whole concept of these teachers, and hamper the educational work that needs to be done with their false claims and distorted messages.[16]

One of the principal problems in attempting to present these ideas to the public is the wrong intellectual focus of so many people, a condition in which the mind has become "the slayer of the Real."[17] We live in a culture—particularly in the Western world—characterized by strong individualism and a rational, scientific, often materialistic mindset. But we are fortunate in that we stand on the verge of discoveries that will help to shatter the dogmas that have perpetrated this limited worldview.

The challenges that will surely confront the teachers as they move outward will be considerable, to say the least. Some people look for a Messiah to solve all problems and alleviate all suffering. That is not what happened two thousand years ago, and we shouldn't think that the situation will be much different today. More often than not, great teachers upset the established order of things. They have always been revolutionaries, and these teachers will be no exception. Their mere presence in the world, with the powerful energy that emanates from both their ideas and their very being, cannot help but upset the status quo. Much as happened two thousand years ago, many people will not accept these teachers and will do all they can to silence the message they come to bring.

And while we should not look to a Messiah to solve our problems, the Ageless Wisdom teachings do state that the coming
teachers, or Masters, are setting the stage and paving the way for
the eventual reemergence of a great World Teacher—a Christ, a
Messiah, a Maitreya, an Imam Mahdi—who comes to unite the
people of the world, to fulfill the prophecy, and to establish a rule
of law upon our planet. According to the Ageless Wisdom teachings, the teacher who is on the way is the Christ. He has not yet
completed the mission he began in Palestine two thousand years
ago and so he comes again, at this dawning of the Aquarian age,
to fulfill the prophecy. But there is a lot of confusion concerning
the word Christ. The Greek "christos" means anointed and, "in the
Greek Mysteries, was applied to a candidate who had passed the
last degree and become a full initiate."[18] In the Ageless Wisdom
teachings, the term Christ refers to the name of an office, the head
of the spiritual Hierarchy.

These distinctions help us come to a deeper understanding of
who this great teacher was and is. Quite a number of people today,
especially within the new age movement, feel a greater connection
and appeal for the Buddha, yet in the fullest sense of the word, the
Buddha and the Christ are the deepest of brothers.

The many distorted perceptions of this great teacher are understandable. The evangelical Christian movement (particularly in
the United States) is exceedingly active—attracting vast numbers
of people and undertaking much good humanitarian work. But in
many ways their teachings have grossly distorted Christ's message,
particularly in regard to his reappearance. It is understandable,
therefore, that many people view Christian teachings as out-of-
touch with progressive living and thinking.

Another picture emerges of this teacher if we read books such
as Huston Smith's, *The World's Religions,* which gives a fascinating
portrait of Jesus the man. Smith's depiction of Christ's life and
work is powerful and conveys a measure of the effect that the actual
physical plane presence of an avatar can have. The facts that we do
know are that he was a "little known Jewish carpenter who was

born in a stable, died at 33 as a criminal rather than a hero, never traveled more than 90 miles from his birthplace, owned nothing, attended no college, marshaled no army, and instead of producing books did his only writing in the sand."

Smith wrote that Christ's greatest influence was upon those closest to him—his disciples, the poor, the prostitutes and the common people. Christ taught that the harlot and the publican may get into heaven before the many who are more outwardly righteous. He empowered the powerless. And we can only speculate about what will happen after his reappearance as the poor still have scant power or sense of entitlement. Surely this is one of the reasons why so many of the disenfranchised people of the world still respond so strongly to his message—for he speaks to them, and few others do.

Christ spoke out against the hypocrisy of his time; he upset the status quo with his words, actions and his very being. And if this was true 2,000 years ago in the relatively isolated world of his ministry in Palestine, can we imagine what an effect his vibration will carry in today's world with its instantaneous global communications network? Due to advances in technology the world has become a much smaller place. People everywhere are being made aware of situations that in the past remained isolated events. The Biblical prophecy that "every ear shall hear and every eye shall see" could easily become a reality in our time. The coming Teacher will take full advantage of this situation, which, by the time he returns, will be even more sophisticated, less expensive, and global in scope. Part of the preparatory work for his return, therefore, involves a stemming of the digital divide so that there will be widespread access to global communications technology.

The prospect of entering this world, with its massive distortions of living and thinking and the coarseness of its vibrations, can surely hold little joy for these teachers. They know the weight of human ignorance and arrogance, but they also know the basic goodness of the human heart. Their intention is to serve humanity, no matter the cost to themselves.[19]

Masculine and Feminine Polarities

Part of the housecleaning that must be completed prior to the teachers' return is related to the need to redress the imbalances in the world by bringing women into positions of prominence in all areas. And this is happening. Women today are demanding full equality—and the essential spiritual equality of all people is the fundamental human right that will provide the underpinning for all the changes that the Aquarian age will usher in. One of the major areas in which women have faced discrimination is the field of religion, which has systematically denied women their full human rights for centuries. This is ironic because many of the founders of these same religions had women prominently placed within their orders. It is therefore a great injustice that women are denied positions of authority today. The ages-old suppression and devaluation of the feminine principle, coupled with economic and racial injustice, stands as the sorriest legacy of the human race. The Aquarian age will see the rectification of this situation, but during the present transition period many difficult challenges must be faced.

The recognition that women are no better than men and men no better than women is a simple truth that is in the process of working out today. In many fields women are emerging as strong leaders, bringing their considerable talents and perspectives to bear upon the important issues of the day. Feminine principles are beginning to be valued and recognized as a necessary component of a just and balanced worldview. But, as in all movements for change, the movement for the liberation of women has resulted in a considerable backlash as many individuals (including many women) fight to maintain the status quo by overtly and covertly devaluing and suppressing women in ways both large and small. Many women, particularly those who live in the developing countries of the world, still suffer gross injustices under the weight of customs born of ignorance and kept in place by fear. A recent United Nations report detailed the abuse to which large numbers of women are subject whether by the state, the family, or strangers—in the public or private sphere, in peacetime or in times of conflict.

Conditions, however, are changing as people change. The overpopulation of the planet is a clear indication that the primary role of woman as child bearer is no longer an evolutionary necessity, and the use of contraceptives has made it possible for many women to turn their energies in other directions. This shift has dramatic implications for women, as it frees them to do much more than was ever possible in the past. This is not meant to devalue women's contribution as child-bearers and mothers; it is simply to state that many other options are open to women today. This freedom, coupled with the fact that both women and men are living much longer, healthier lives, is giving us all increased opportunities to contribute in new and exciting ways.

Perhaps in our short-sightedness we think that because women have made great strides within the workplace and have entered into the professional world in increasing numbers, there is no further progress to be made. But we all know that fundamental change is that which takes place in attitude, and we have a long way to go before women will be afforded the respect and dignity they deserve. The new age will see a change in the attitude of men towards women and of women towards their destiny.[20] This will work out most noticeably in the areas of sex and marriage. As men learn to value women, women will be freed to realize their spiritual destiny. That destiny is in process of unfolding under the impetus of the inflowing energy of Aquarius, but surely woman's destiny will be uniquely her own—different, yet complementary to that of men. The feminine perspective, which is overwhelmingly a voice in support of peace and justice, is still devalued in our world with the disastrous results that we witness all around us.

It is helpful to remember that we all experience many lifetimes in both male and female bodies as we pass through the long series of lives that constitute the path of human evolution. This fact helps to explain the different orientations that occur frequently when, for example, an individual has passed a series of lives in one sex and then enters into incarnation in the opposite polarity. The Law of Rebirth helps us develop a deepened understanding of life's many complexities. We all incarnate in each gender to gain experience and develop different qualities. The Ageless Wisdom teaches that the polarity of women and men is quite different on an energetic level. Of course there are no hard and fast rules and lines of demarcation, and as we enter Aquarius there appears to be a great blending and fusing of the sexes taking place as we move into a deeper understanding of equality. But from the perspective of essential polarity men are positive, while women are "negative" or receptive. Traditionally these polarities have led to the devaluation and consequent suppression of women. But as the energies of the new age come into increasing dominance, there will be a deepened understanding of equality that will embrace our differences. This will give place to a fuller understanding with a resultant greater harmony between the sexes.

Women have a vital and integral part to play in the work that is being done today and take their place within the forefront of the planetary changes that are unfolding in all departments of living. In a certain sense, because of their receptivity, women possess a great openness to impression from the inner teachers and can be receivers from the spiritual worlds. As a consequence, many of the people who have been instrumental in shaping and forging the spiritual movement have been women.

The Ageless Wisdom teaches, however, that people who reach the fifth degree of initiation—that of a Master of the Wisdom—do so in a male body. This is not meant to signify that men are better than women, to repeat, we all pass through a myriad of lives in both sexes. But traditionally it has been taught that a male body is necessary to withstand the enormity of the challenges confronting those who have attained the fifth degree. However, in relationship to this, there was an interesting comment made by H.H. the Dalai Lama in response to a question posed to him by Pir Zia, head of the Sufi Order International. While studying with His Holiness in Dharamsala, India a number of years ago, Pir Zia asked, "Is it really true that women cannot attain Buddhahood?" His Holiness responded, "This was true until Tara became a bodhisattva."[21] He went on to say, "Tara was the world's first feminist." So perhaps even in this area of long-held tradition there are no longer any hard and fast rules. This delicate question is, therefore, left for future consideration.

CHAPTER 2

A BRIEF HISTORICAL PERSPECTIVE

THE FOUNDING OF THE HIERARCHY ON EARTH

When we consider these things in light of the situation in the world today, many questions will naturally arise. We might wonder, for example, "If these teachers exist, why is there so much suffering in the world? Why were conditions allowed to become so dire; why don't these teachers step forward and set things right? Why would they allow such conditions to exist?" These are good questions. They can perhaps partially be answered by briefly considering the situation in the light of the Ageless Wisdom teachings. This perspective recedes far back into the annals of time—to a period that antedates all recorded history but has been carried down to us in myth, legend, and ancient spiritual texts that have, in some cases, been preserved in the protected places of the world. What follows is an extremely fragmentary and rudimentary presentation of teachings that are developed in considerable detail and depth in the writings of Helena Blavatsky (particularly *Isis Unveiled* and *The Secret Doctrine*), which can be studied to great benefit by anyone who is interested in gaining a deeper understanding of the history of our planetary life from the perspective of the Ageless Wisdom teachings. This material is adapted from the chapter titled "The Founding of the Hierarchy," taken from *Initiation, Human and Solar*.

According to those teachings the spiritual Hierarchy first established itself upon our planet some eighteen-and-a-half million years ago when the infinitely great Being, Sanat Kumara, came here to undertake a great work of sacrifice and redemption. He is said to be a being of such incredible purity (relatively sinless) that he was unable to take a physical body and was only able to function in an etheric or energy body. Everything within the world is said to be held within His aura or magnetic sphere of influence.

Sanat Kumara came to our planet with a group of other highly evolved entities in order to carry out a great plan that has been unfolding all these millions of years. Only now (within the coming centuries), with the developments that are coming into play, will these entities begin to see the realization and fruition of the work they came to do so very long ago.

When Sanat Kumara first came here, the world was full of animal men who had highly evolved physical bodies, coordinated astral bodies, and the rudimentary germ of mind. If left alone, these creatures would have eventually evolved out of the animal kingdom and into the human, but it would have been an exceedingly long, slow process. Sanat Kumara's decision to take on a higher physical (etheric) vehicle was a tremendously important event in the evolutionary life of our planet. It produced an extraordinary inflow of spiritual energy that stimulated the evolutionary process. All forms of life were enlivened by the energy pouring through them and emanating from this great Life, this Silent Watcher.

The germ of mind in animal man was stimulated and as a result led to an opportunity for a great step forward to be taken; this is called "individualization" in the spiritual books and signifies the process of moving these animal beings into the human kingdom through mental stimulation. This "fecundation" of the brains of these animal men was brought about by an advanced group of extra-planetary beings known in the teachings as the Solar Angels.

Even after this great event, ages came and went and the work of the Hierarchy proceeded at an exceedingly slow and discouraging pace, without much progress of any kind. Then, about seventeen million years ago, it was decided that an outpost of the Hierarchy was needed upon the dense physical plane that would serve as a type of organization and headquarters for the ancient mysteries. This Hierarchy would be run by a band of Masters and Chohans who would function in dense physical bodies to better meet the need of the world.[22]

The first location of the Hierarchy was found in the center of South America, in what was known as the Temple of Ibez. Another location was found in the ancient Mayan civilization. A second branch was later established in Asia, known as the Trans-Himalayan School, and this model still governs the work of the Hierarchy today.[23] Much later, during the time of the Atlantean civilization, the great teachers walked openly among humanity and held the reins of power and authority in that ancient time.[24] Their civilization possessed an in-depth knowledge in many fields such as mathematics, architecture and philosophy—some of which remains largely unknown to this day. But over time the people of Atlantis became overwhelmed by the material and emotional forces that, in time, led to their destruction, and the teachers had to withdraw from outer activity.[25] At about this time certain members of the human kingdom were making such strides in their evolutionary development that the entire constitution of the Hierarchy was shifting to accommodate this human achievement.

The legend of the great flood that has come down to us was an actual event that took place during that distant time of Atlantis.[26] As a result of this terrible destruction, the teachers re-evaluated their position with regard to the human family (and their own evolution) and came to the decision that they needed to change the way in which they worked.[27] They decided that it was no longer appropriate to work openly as the protectors of humanity. Humanity, it was felt, needed to learn the lessons of freedom and self-determination, and so the teachers withdrew. After a time, humanity lost its conscious recollection of them.

Ever since that distant time, humanity has largely been left free. We humans have created the problems and we have to solve them. As we do, the teachers will return and we will again be given the opportunity for true spiritual leadership upon the physical plane. The teachers are not coming so much to lead but rather to walk with us so that together we can reorient the entire tone and pulse of our planetary life.

MESSENGERS OF THE LIGHT

Over the past 130 years many different individuals have helped to bring the concept of the Masters of the Wisdom to public attention. The following brief listing is by no means exhaustive—many other individuals and groups, often working quietly behind the scenes, have helped to solidify this teaching in the world.

Helena Petrovna Blavatsky

> The Buddha has said: ...that we must not believe in a thing said merely because it is said; nor traditions because they have been handed down from antiquity; nor rumours, as such; nor writings by sages because sages wrote them; nor fancies that we may suspect to have been inspired in us by a Deva (that is, in presumed spiritual inspiration); nor from inferences drawn from some haphazard assumption we have made; nor because of what seems an analogical necessity; nor on the mere authority of teachers or masters. But we are to believe when the writing, doctrine, or saying is corroborated by our own reading and consciousness. 'For this,' He says in concluding, 'I taught you not to believe merely because you have heard, but when believed of your own consciousness, then to act accordingly and abundantly.'
>
> Helena Blavatsky, *The Secret Doctrine*

Madame Blavatsky, as she was called, could very well be viewed as the "mother" of the whole movement to bring the Ageless Wisdom teaching to the West. She was the one who, with her strength, courage and depth of knowledge, paved the way for everything that has followed. We are all deeply indebted to her work and the sacrifices she made to bring into the light some of the secrets of the ages that until then had been largely lost and hidden in the modern world. She knew full well that her writings would be scorned by those who did not have eyes to see. But she continued nonetheless to the end of her days to bring forward the fruits of her knowledge.

Mme. Blavatsky was a colorful, flamboyant Russian woman who lived and worked at the end of the nineteenth century. Her brilliant writings, especially *The Secret Doctrine* and *Isis Unveiled*, as well as her co-founding of the Theosophical Society, made her quite famous, and sometimes infamous, in her day. Her work was instrumental in setting this movement upon a sound footing, one that attracted some of the leading figures of the day to its ranks and brought articles related to the Masters into many major newspapers.

At a young age Blavatsky set out to learn all she could about the ancient mysteries—from books and life experience as well as by her own abilities to penetrate into the inner worlds. She traveled widely, throughout Europe and to Egypt and India, where she actually lived and trained with certain Masters in preparation for the later work that she would do. Blavatsky was in constant contact with these teachers via letter and in physical and inner plane experiences. They were instrumental in helping her with both her writing and the formation of the Theosophical Society, which was a major event on the global scene during its early days. Blavatsky's work was misunderstood by some of the people of her time, leading her to regret ever having mentioned the Masters.[28] She was viciously attacked and maligned, and she suffered greatly under the weight of this criticism, but her work helped to prepare human consciousness for the events that are now beginning to unfold.

Annie Besant

> Never forget that life can only be nobly inspired and rightly lived if you take it bravely and gallantly, as a splendid adventure in which you are setting out into an unknown country, to meet many a joy, to find many a comrade, to win and lose many a battle.
>
> Annie Besant

Annie Besant, the British writer, feminist, lecturer and humanitarian, worked tirelessly to promote the cause of the Ageless Wisdom teachings. As a young woman she made a complete break with her Christian upbringing and, through the 1880s, worked actively in the socialist movement in England and became a powerful advocate for women's rights. Then, in 1889, she joined the Theosophical Society, a move that she said shocked even her closest friends. She went on to become its second President, from 1907 until her death in 1933. She spent most of this time in India, where she also continued her interest in politics and women's suffrage. She worked with Gandhi who considered her one of the key figures in "awakening India from her deep slumber." Mrs. Besant led the Hindu nationalist movement, founded Central Hindu College and organized the Indian Home Rule League. She was even elected president of the Indian National Congress in 1917 and general secretary of the National Convention of India in 1923.

She was the author of over forty books and was a highly regarded lecturer in both East and West. She sponsored the work of the young Indian boy Jiddhu Krishnamurti, adopted him in 1911 and was responsible for his education in England. The stimulation surrounding her involvement with the Krishnamurti "experiment" may have contributed to the errors in judgment that surrounded some of her activities within the Theosophical Society during her later years. These errors do not, however, diminish her full life of service to the Plan of the Hierarchy as she understood it.

Jiddhu Krishnamurti

> One-pointedness means ... that nothing shall ever turn you, even for a moment, from the Path upon which you have entered. No temptations, no worldly pleasures, no worldly affections even, must ever draw you aside. For you yourself must become one with the Path; it must be so much part of your nature that you follow it without needing to think of it, and cannot turn aside. You, the Monad, have decided it; to break away from it would be to break away from yourself.
>
> J. Krishnamurti, *At the Feet of the Master*

In the early years of the twentieth century, certain members of the Theosophical Society in India proclaimed a young Indian boy, Jiddu Krishnamurti, to be the incarnation of a great spiritual teacher. And indeed Krishnamurti was a very special youth. Many people who became acquainted with him during those early years attested to his rare spiritual gifts and to his purity. People who heard Krishnamurti speak were spiritually uplifted and he attracted the attention of a wide range of individuals merely by his presence and the strength and inherent truth that his words conveyed. He spoke openly of his relationship with the Masters and showed himself to be impressed from the inner planes. His life was a manifestation of truth.

The Bailey teachings state that Krishnamurti was an experiment in what is called "overshadowing." This word is bandied about quite freely today as many people claim themselves to be channels for the Masters. One must therefore be discriminating and separate truth from falsity when considering such claims. But in the case of Krishnamurti, there is little doubt that the influence of the Masters worked through him. He was, in a sense, able to give over his own lower personality vehicles so that the Masters could bring their influence to bear upon the world through the person of Krishnamurti.[29] During such moments of overshadowing it was as if Krishnamurti, through an interior process of alignment, was able to allow his vehicles to become the channel for the inflowing light and power of energies that were much greater than his own normal level of development. On a higher turn of the spiral, this is what happened within the life of Jesus, whose purity of life and intention enabled the Christ to work through him.

Unfortunately, the people who had Krishnamurti's well-being and care within their hands proclaimed him to be the next world teacher, which ignited a fury around this delicate experiment that was being attempted. Some members of the Theosophical Society, who really had done some wonderful work, lost their way with the Krishnamurti experience and were unable to handle the responsibility that had been given to them. As Krishnamurti matured, an organization, "The Order of the Star of the East," formed around him and he attracted a large following. Unfortunately, the whole phenomenon became a cult of personality and Krishnamurti was placed upon a pedestal. The distortions and the misplaced devotion naturally caused a great revolt within Krishnamurti. In 1929, in front of a crowd of three thousand he gave his famous speech in which he asserted that "Truth is a pathless land" and effectively disbanded the entire movement. Krishnamurti had had enough of religion, dogma and doctrines. Rebelling against the devotion that had swelled up around him, he no longer spoke of the Hierarchy publicly.

As a result, the experiment that the Masters were attempting to undertake was withdrawn. The inner conditions within Krishnamurti changed, and the Masters no longer worked through him. The experiment was not a complete failure, however, and surely some valuable lessons were learned by all involved. Krishnamurti went on to do much good work of a spiritual nature along the lines of education and the spiritual life—but one cannot help but wonder how the experiment might have worked out differently had the individuals responsible for nurturing the young Krishnamurti handled the situation differently and acted with greater wisdom and care.

The problems that arose within the Theosophical Society and within the many people who were drawn to Krishnamurti can give us a glimpse into the emotionally charged situations that surround highly evolved souls and warn of the difficulties that can arise when the Masters externalize. The problems confronting Krishnamurti seem to have arisen out of his reaction to the intense devotion directed toward him. This is particularly interesting because devotion is the primary quality associated with the passing Piscean age and the accompanying energy of the sixth ray. In a sense, then, Krishnamurti could be viewed as reacting in an appropriate manner for one who is coming under the influence of the Aquarian energies, which relate strongly to the concept of freedom. But as a result of his reaction to the situation in which he found himself, it seems Krishnamurti closed down his own channel to hierarchical impression.

While individuals of Krishnamurti's stature are uncommon, there are many people who bring Hierarchical energy to bear upon the work that they do while involved in speaking, creating, writing, or organizational planning. These, in fact, are the primary means by which the Hierarchy works at this time, prior to the actual return of the Masters themselves. The Masters demonstrate the utmost humility as they serve without recognition for the work that they do. They receive no credit or accolades from the outer world, yet they stand silently behind many of the beautiful and creative inspirations that emerge from humanity.[30]

Rudolf Steiner

> Man is effective in the world not only through what he does, but above all through what he is.
>
> Rudolf Steiner

Steiner was another important teacher who came out of the Theosophical tradition and did much to bring forward its concepts. He was an exceptionally erudite man who was, among other things, a philosopher, a writer and a lecturer. He founded the Anthroposophical Society, which continues to offer classes and workshops related to different aspects of Steiner's work. His ideas had a strong influence in the fields of spirituality, architectural design, medicine, agriculture, and pre-eminently in education, through the Waldorf schools. In his almost thirty books and over six thousand lectures, Steiner taught extensively about the spiritual Hierarchy and the inner worlds and the ways by which we can begin to contact them.

Helena and Nicholas Roerich

> All preceding Yogas, given from the highest Sources, took as their basis a definite quality of life. And now, at the advent of the age of Maitreya there is needed a Yoga comprising the essence of the entire life, all-embracing, evading nought.... You may suggest to Me a name for the Yoga of life. But the most precise name will be Agni Yoga. It is precisely the element of Fire which gives to this Yoga of self-sacrifice its name.... Fire, as an all-binding element, manifests itself everywhere and thereby admits realisation of the subtlest energies. The fire will not lead away from life; it will act as a trustworthy guide into the far-off worlds.
>
> *Agni Yoga*, 158

Helena and Nicholas Roerich were Russian by birth and their primary work was undertaken during the first half of the twentieth century. They were both writers and spiritual teachers; Nicholas was also a prolific painter. Helena brought forth what has come to be known as the Agni Yoga teachings. These collections of short spiritual aphorisms have helped many people by means of the "straight-knowledge" they transmit through poetic, spiritual imagery. This is a first ray teaching inspired by the Master Morya. The teachings, as well as Roerich's paintings, have given much to the world through their beauty and wisdom inspired from the higher worlds. The Roerichs founded the Agni Yoga Society in New York which publishes and handles all of the administrative work and also serves as a museum for some of Nicholas Roerich's paintings. The Roerichs were also instrumental in formulating the "Banner of Peace" project, which continues today to promote peace and brotherhood in the world.

Alice Bailey

The twenty books written by Alice Bailey in cooperation with the Tibetan contain much of the teaching for the new age. Central to this teaching is information about the Masters. When Bailey was fifteen years old, she was contacted by her Master, Koot Humi, an occurrence that is described in her *Unfinished Autobiography*.[31] She was home alone one day reading when suddenly a tall, turbaned Indian man entered into the room. Bailey's initial reaction was one of fear, but as he spoke directly and seriously to her, she was compelled to pay attention. The basic intent of this "interview" was to let her know that she had special work to do, but that in order to accomplish it she would have to make certain major personality changes. At that time, having grown up in the conservatism and shelter of an upper-class British family at the end of the nineteenth century, Bailey was extremely bad-tempered and rather contemptuous of other people. She also considered beneath her those who did not adhere to her Christian faith. As a result of the powerful impact that her contact with her Master made upon her, Bailey successfully made the changes asked of her and went on to live a very full life of service.

Bailey attained a level of awareness that enabled her to work in conscious contact with the Masters regarding the work she had to do, and her relationship with them lasted the rest of her life. She rarely talked about this contact, as there is an unstated code of silence about this inner work and Bailey always maintained a high degree of humility. She was concerned with the work that she came to do and not so much with herself as an individual.

Bailey was an extremely hard-working woman who raised three daughters, wrote twenty books for the Tibetan as well as four books of her own, and founded the *Beacon* magazine. She and her husband, Foster Bailey, also founded the Lucis Trust, which continues to this day with headquarters in New York, London and Geneva. She also developed the curriculum of the Arcane School, which is a long-term correspondence course that has served spiritual seekers throughout the world for over eighty years. Bailey traveled and lectured widely as well as meeting and corresponding with literally thousands of people who sought her out wherever she went. She worked with a seasoned and trusted group of coworkers, without whose help she would have been unable to carry forward her work.

When the Tibetan teacher contacted Bailey through a deep subjective experience and sought her cooperation in the work of writing his books, she flatly refused to help him. She said that she wanted no part of any psychic work. The Tibetan told her that the books that he hoped to bring forward to the public with her help could provide a real service to others. He asked her to consider the idea for one month, and if after that time she still didn't want to work with him, he would attempt to find someone else.[32]

Bailey later reported in her autobiography that she promptly forgot all about the whole experience. She was the mother of three small children at the time and was actively involved with the work of the Krotona Theosophical Society in California. When the Tibetan contacted her a month later, she again expressed her displeasure with the idea. She felt a deep distrust of the type of work that she thought was being asked of her. This time the Tibetan suggested that she try working with him for a month to better enable her to evaluate the quality of the teaching.

But after taking the dictation for a month-long period, Bailey still refused to continue with the work. She worried that if the work adversely affected her in any way, there would be no one to care for her girls. The Tibetan suggested that she contact her own Master and discuss the matter with him. Bailey did this (upon the inner planes) and found that it was indeed her Master who had suggested her for this project in the first place. He assured her that this work would not cause any harm to her and that her girls would be safe. She finally agreed and continued the work on the series of instructions that eventually became known as the book *Initiation, Human and Solar*. From the beginning the Tibetan had said that their work would last for thirty years, and indeed it began in

November 1919 and continued until Bailey's death in December 1949.

The Master Djwhal Khul's books cover a wide array of subjects, including teaching on the seven rays, healing, astrology, psychology, initiation, the Hierarchy, meditation and telepathy. Bailey took down the teaching by a process of mental telepathy that she developed with the Tibetan. She then formulated the writings into the proper phrasing and a type of English suitable to the times. The books are not, therefore, her own thoughts and ideas. All of the information was carefully reviewed and revised by the Tibetan himself to assure that it was an accurate reflection of his intention. The Tibetan stated that Alice Bailey's cooperation was invaluable to the work that he brought forth. Although the books were published under Alice Bailey's name, she never claimed the teaching as her own.

The manner by which the books were written has understandably caused considerable interest and questioning in the minds of many people over the years. When Carl Jung was given some of the Bailey material, for example, he said he did not believe that the books were transmitted from a Tibetan through a process of mental telepathy. He thought, instead, that the writings were the product of Bailey's subconscious mind and that the Tibetan was the embodiment of her higher consciousness.[33] Bailey, however, knew otherwise. She responded that she had written entire treatises upon subjects of which she knew absolutely nothing.

The Tibetan is said to be one of the most learned of all the Masters and is sometimes called the "Messenger," as he has assumed responsibility for bringing forth teaching for the Hierarchy as a whole. And while much of that information is clearly well beyond the comprehension of many people today, as mentioned, it contains only a fraction of the Tibetan's depth of understanding. Bailey spoke with amazement of the glimpses of limitless vistas of spiritual truth that she obtained through her collaboration with the Tibetan—truth that she could not possibly have otherwise contacted and of a quality she could not possibly express. The

Tibetan was also said to have cooperated with Helena Blavatsky in her writing of *The Secret Doctrine* and *Isis Unveiled*.[34] The books indicate that there will be yet a third installment or continuation of the teaching given out over the next decades through another amanuensis.[35]

CHAPTER 3

LIFE AFTER LIFE

... each life is not only a recapitulation of life experience, but an assuming of ancient obligations, a recovery of old relations, an opportunity for the paying of old indebtedness, a chance to make restitution and progress, an awakening of deep-seated qualities, the recognition of old friends and enemies, the solution of revolting injustices, and the explanation of that which conditions the man and makes him what he is.

Alice Bailey, *Esoteric Psychology, Vol. I*

THE LAW OF REBIRTH

Considerable debate often arises when the subject of reincarnation is addressed. Generally it is rejected vehemently by those with a materialistic mindset who ridicule anything outside the bounds of their individual experience. And the fundamentalists reject out-of-hand any worldview that fails to correspond to their dogma. But the open-minded and searching individual will generally reserve judgment.

One of the primary teachings that the new age will usher in will be a clarification of the Law of Rebirth. This teaching will do so much to elevate human consciousness. We'll come to understand that all action generates karma—either positive or negative, depending upon the qualifying motive that underlies it. This recognition will help us to tread more carefully the path of life.

We'll understand that whatever we sow, so shall we reap, and we "will reap it here and now, and not in some mystical and mythical heaven or hell."[36]

As we come to understand the cyclic nature of all life, we realize that nothing within the universe is static—all forms are constantly mutating, recapitulating and evolving to ever higher states of being through a ceaseless process of life, death and rebirth. Evolution is the one constant—there is no ending point, no final goal, no ultimate destination that we eventually achieve and then rest on our laurels.

Instead, each of us is a work in progress. Over the course of many lifetimes filled with joys and sorrows, we each have the opportunity to weave an intricate and beautiful tapestry out of the materials that are given to us, a tapestry that is ever a reflection of who or what we essentially are. Lifetime to lifetime we round out our essential nature by adding new colors and deepening the existing hues. In each life the soul picks up the thread of past activities and associations. And in this journey, there are always forks upon the way and detours that may slow us down and take us in a different direction. Sometimes these lead to crisis points and consequent periods of indecision and loss of clarity that can cause us to lose our way for a time. These experiences should give us pause and an interlude for reflection from which we will eventually take our next step.

The teaching on rebirth is, of course, nothing new. It has been accepted by many people, especially in the East, throughout the ages. Unfortunately it has often been misinterpreted and distorted. For example, some schools of thought teach that someone who commits wrong action in a particular lifetime then might be forced to reincarnate in the form of an animal or an insect in the next lifetime. This is a distortion of the law that teaches the forward progression of all life forms into ever higher states of consciousness. And while there is a karmic debt (a price to pay) for wrong action, it does not involve reincarnation in the animal world.

People have sometimes responded to teachings about rebirth by abandoning their will to fate. For example, the archaic caste system that Gandhi tried to break (and which is still in place in certain parts of India) was a direct result of a misinterpretation of this law. The thinking goes that since the path is long and there are many lifetimes ahead of each one of us, we should accept our fate and be content with our station in life. People who adopt such an attitude risk being taken advantage of by others. It is, of course, true that one lifetime is largely insignificant when viewed from the long-range perspective of the soul. But it is equally true that each lifetime and, in fact, each day is an opportunity that can be made spiritually significant depending upon the quality of living-ness that we bring to it. So while there is no need to rush, there is likewise no time to lose—especially during times of planetary emergency such as the present.

Another problem that can cloud understanding of the Law of Rebirth stems from the consideration of past lives. While it is natural to be curious about this subject as we begin to accept the possibility of reincarnation, most people only have vague recollections about the past, and information provided by others is generally suspect and not subject to verification.

Sometimes traumas from past lives still haunt us in the present. We have all passed through difficult experiences, not only in this lifetime, but also in the past. These events can contribute to the sometimes vague fears that arise from deep within us—fears that we can't really understand because they relate to our unconscious experience. These fears can sometimes limit our ability to express our higher self, yet they are difficult to alleviate because they re-main intangible and vague within our conscious minds. We can create problems for ourselves, however, by attempting to delve too deeply into the vast pool of the subconscious through such tech-niques as past life regression, hypnosis, and too much attention to the dream life, all of which can bring up information and aggravate conditions that would best be left alone. If we work with highly skilled people, relief can sometimes be found via these channels, but caution is essential.

The past is shielded from us for a reason, and it's best to be respectful of the soul's wisdom. We all have gifts and talents, developed over the course of many lifetimes, that become the means of overcoming the shadows—propelling us forward into the light. These gifts free us to give what is ours to give. All things will eventually be revealed, and we will be given the necessary tools to uncover the history of our past and the prospect of our future lives, but until such time we can rest content with the fleeting intimations that come upon us. Too often psychics give out misinformation relating to past lives of fame and glory when the truth might be quite the reverse.

It's common today among New Age types to hear people state that they do not want to return to this Earth plane. They say that they have had enough pain and suffering, that they've paid their dues. But release from the wheel of rebirth is not that easy; if it were, many more people would have achieved the goal. The path of growth into spiritual consciousness is long; it takes many, many lives before we can even begin to see the goal, which is only one of a series of goals stretching out before us without end.

The path, however, is infinitely more complex than a simple forward trajectory through a long series of lives that mysteriously transport us into the region of the higher realms. Changes in consciousness depend wholly upon the nature of our individual efforts and striving, upon the fine tuning of our life and the ability to persist and stand firm amidst the inevitable obstacles and suffering. Change comes slowly, and often it seems that as we take one step forward, in the next moment we might find ourselves having to take two steps back. And it is infinitely harder still to reach the level of attainment of a Master of the Wisdom.

The great teachers have all passed, as do we, through the rounds of birth and death. They are each the result of a long series of lives of discipline and sacrifice that lead, eventually, to the attainment of successive points of enlightenment upon the never-ending spiral that is the path of return. The exacting nature of that path is implicit in the definition of an adept as the "rare efflorescence of a generation of inquirers."[37] This definition should give us pause and deepen our understanding of the very real achievement of the great teachers. But because of our limitations in consciousness, we cannot comprehend fully the distinction that exists between the Masters and ourselves—in a similar fashion that an animal is completely unable to comprehend the complexities and subtleties that make up a human being.

The Masters have wrestled and fought their way into a greater measure of light, and Their effort should inspire us to want to do the same, even as we falter many times along the way. They possess a more complete understanding of the Law of Rebirth than we possibly can, and we can learn from their experience and their patience. They understand more fully the relativity of time and space and view life and its events from a long-range perspective, with an extended vision, rather than from the confines of a few short years or lifetimes. And, as a consequence, they reserve judgment. Their observations of their students, for example, take place at long intervals. They don't concern themselves with the petty details of their students' lives—with their faults or their so-called successes—and consequently leave them free. Events are viewed differently from the perspective of the inner planes, and we can begin to develop this perspective by cultivating a sense of the eternal amidst the tumult of daily life.

The Buddha and the Christ stand as models to us all to follow—the Buddha because of the wisdom of his teaching on detachment, discrimination and dispassion, and the Christ because of the depth of his sacrifice and the teaching on the nature of cosmic love. In the long history of our planet no one ever moved forward as quickly on the path as did Christ.[38] But because of the nature of this particular planetary cycle, many individuals are now beginning to evolve at a similarly rapid rate. It is as if by merely being alive and striving, many more people than ever before are being presented with unprecedented spiritual opportunities.

Ultimately the choice of a rapid or slow evolutionary development is ours. No one, no outer teacher, no guru or spiritual sage, can do more than point the way for us. Neither can any teaching really influence or change us at fundamental levels if we have not yet made certain inner decisions. But once we have made those decisions, nothing can stop us as we move into alignment with our soul. We each, therefore, have a choice: we can take the long, slow route of normal evolutionary growth and development and we will eventually reach the goal or, through our individual efforts, we can take the path of conscious return and enter within that "forcing process" that will carry us forward with greater speed and confidence into the light. The goal of this accelerated progress is the increased capacity to serve. Each one of us holds within us all the resources necessary to make this shift. It is up to us.

DEATH: THE GREAT LIBERATION

> One day we will learn that death cannot steal
> Anything gained by the soul.
>
> Rabindranath Tagore

A deeper understanding of death will help to lead humanity onto the road to liberation. That is why certain people, such as church leaders, have feared this knowledge throughout time and tried to keep it hidden. If the authority of one's own soul is recognized, it lessens the grip of the outer authorities and weakens their power. The thinning of the veils that separate the inner and outer worlds is gradually bringing about a revolution in human thinking about death and a recognition of the essential unity of all forms of consciousness and states of being. The traditional Christian teaching on death doesn't satisfy anymore. It seems doubtful, for example, that a loving and compassionate God would condemn people to eternal damnation.

The Buddhist perspective on death is more aligned with reality. Buddhists believe the moment of death to be one of supreme opportunity. In fact, the Buddhist tradition teaches that from certain angles, our entire life could be viewed as a preparation for the moment of death, when it is possible for a great expansion of consciousness to occur. The Buddhist teachings provide a real service in their focus upon the need to prepare oneself throughout one's life for the moment of death by living mindfully, practicing loving-kindness, and making the attempt to be ready, at any moment, to leave this world with a prepared consciousness. The Tibetan teacher Sogyal Rinpoche's *Tibetan Book of Living and Dying* provides a wealth of insight into the process of dying as well as some fascinating accounts of the deaths of a number of enlightened Buddhist monks.

Many other people today do not believe in any type of afterlife at all and instead tend to view death as little more than a long sleep. And, in certain ways, the comparison is not far from the mark. It only holds true, however, if we come to view sleep from a deeper perspective. For in reality, little is known about sleep other than its physiological aspects and a rudimentary understanding of dreams. But there is much more to sleep than that.

The veils between the inner and outer world are composed of etheric matter. These veils block and protect us, during our waking consciousness, from information that we are not yet capable of assimilating. Each night, however, we pierce through them as we exit our body and move freely within another dimension of reality. It is from this dimension that our most significant dreams emanate and from which we can, at times, receive fleeting, deep impressions, or recollections, of a more profound reality.

During our time of sleep, our spirit enters into this well-known world with its various activities and responsibilities. We work with others, some of whom we may know and others who are unknown in our waking consciousness. It is this group that we can most accurately call our "group brothers." The work that we undertake upon the inner planes is uniquely designed to make use of our

specific talents and gifts, as we each have our tasks and assign-
ments to fulfill within the great scheme of things, but we do so
alongside, and in the closest cooperation with, our group brothers.
It is this inner association that occurs during the hours of sleep
that so often accounts for the immediate sense of recognition that
sometimes takes place when we actually meet one of these people
for the first time upon the physical plane, perhaps as a new friend
or coworker. Although the relationship seems new and intriguing
to us at the time, it is really old and well-established because of the
shared work and responsibilities that already exist upon the inner
planes. The depth of the inner bond will be revealed through time
and association as it works out upon the physical plane.

Death is a mystery to most of us, and our lack of clarity related
to it is the cause of much pain and suffering. One of the greatest
successes of those who seek to hold back the forces of evolution
upon our planet has been this fostering of the fear of death.[39] So
much needless suffering results both for the dying individual and
for his or her friends and family as a result of misperceptions
about death. The fear of death, paradoxically, distorts our life. We
do all we can to prolong life, and in the process our values become
distorted by an over-idealization of youth. A massive industry, at
a cost of billions of dollars, has built up around the desire to stave
off the inevitable and the true fruits of age; a garnered wisdom
that should be our legacy to the young, atrophies because our attention is deflected away from things of the spirit, and everyone
suffers as a result.

This preservation of the body at all costs works out in particularly harmful ways when it comes to the modern ways of dealing
with death and the dying. The medical profession, divorced from
spiritual considerations, takes on endless procedures to prolong
lives that, in many cases, should just be allowed to pass on, once
there is no hope and the body and brain are obviously deterio-
rating. Allowing people to die more natural deaths would save
millions of dollars in health care costs and untold suffering. But
when it comes to a question of euthanasia, we are confronted with

a delicate situation, primarily because of our lack of understanding of the laws of death and the intentions of the soul. When we come to understand more fully the spiritual dimensions of life, we will know that death comes at its own moment just as surely as birth. It is important to have legal safeguards related to death, but the Tibetan wrote, "Where, however, there is terrible suffering and absolutely no hope of real help or recovery, and where the patient is willing (or if too ill, the family is willing), then, under proper safeguards, something should be done." [40]

The embalming of bodies is another practice that is harmful to the intentions of the soul, as it impedes the ability of the etheric body to make a smooth and graceful transition into the higher realms. At death it is the etheric connection with the physical that is severed and released into the great reservoir of life. When a body is embalmed, this process of release is hindered. Cremation is, therefore, a much healthier and spiritually correct means of disposing of bodies. Also, the continual burying of diseased bodies has contaminated the soil of our planet. The Ageless Wisdom teachings state that syphilis (and consequently AIDS, which is a derivative of the syphilitic diseases) is, in fact, extremely ancient in origin and actually related to this contamination of the soil. This problem of the soil could be rectified through the practice of cremation. [41]

The apparent separation that death brings is only due to our limitations within consciousness, to our circumscribed perceptions, and not to the reality of the situation. When we are attending to a dying person and we attempt to center ourselves in the light, in this way helping him or her to do the same, we aid the departing soul in making a smooth and fearless transition. We can become, in a very real sense, the "midwives" of death. But to become effective in this work is a challenge—one that involves a reorientation of our own attitudes towards the dying person and towards death itself. As we come to understand the fallacy inherent in the distorted perceptions of death, we will recognize that there is no real separation between ourselves and those who have passed over.

The dying do not usually suffer from our accustomed limitations, as they are moving in a new direction. It is often the attachments and the fears of loved ones that "hold" people to the earth plane when what they really need to do is let go and move forward into the next realm of consciousness. We could do our loved ones a favor by practicing detachment and thereby aiding them in their transition. Even after death we can continue to assist the departed one during the transition period. It takes time for the process of dying to be completed and for the soul to fully let go of its vehicles. In the not too distant future we will come to recognize death as a triumphant finale to life and as a more joyous occasion than a birth or marriage.[42] This is not to say that we will not miss our departed friends or loved ones. But we should be happy for them and for the release that they have achieved and know that we will be reunited with them again.

Due to advances in medical technology during recent decades, increasing numbers of people have reported passing through "near-death" experiences. These reports have done much to bring to light information related to death. Some people question the validity of these experiences and whether what occurred was truly related to death, or just a type of hallucinatory experience of some sort. But these reports, because of their striking similarity to each other, have become increasingly difficult to ignore. Near-death accounts are doing much to help shatter fears of death, for overwhelmingly the experience is reported as a beautiful and joyous release from the restrictions of form life as well as a reunion with spiritual teachers, friends, loved ones and pets. Anyone who has read Ken Wilber's account in *Grace and Grit* of his wife Treya's death will recognize her "spiritual" death experience as one of great release and, in fact, joy.

The Tibetan teacher gave us a few interesting insights into death, and it may prove helpful to summarize some of them here. His primary point was that death should not be feared. It is governed by the law of cycles and unfolds in alignment with the intentions of the overshadowing soul.

He asks that we begin to give more thought to the process of dying. This is surely happening to many people today, particularly among those who are working within the hospice movement and among those researchers who are beginning to attempt a more scientific investigation into near-death experiences. The following summary of remarks from the Tibetan apply to those cases when an individual has suffered and is now clearly dying with no hope of recovery.

Death differs from the process of sleep; at death there is a withdrawal of the two threads of energy—the one that is anchored in the head, called the consciousness thread, and the other, known as the life thread, which is anchored in the heart. At the time of sleep it is only the thread in the head that withdraws. Preparation for death, we learn, is a lifelong process. The primary means of preparation that we can undertake is the attempt to control our emotional natures and orient our minds towards things spiritual.

The following points will aid the dying person. The first suggestion is to maintain silence in the death chamber. Although the dying patient appears to be without any consciousness, nevertheless consciousness is there. Silence enables the departing soul to take possession of the body and make due preparations for the transition into death. It is suggested that orange lights will facilitate the withdrawal from the physical body, as orange is said to aid the focusing in the head. Also, it will be found that certain types of music will be used to aid in the abstracting process as well as pressure on certain nerve centers and arteries. Some of these techniques are preserved in the books on dying from Tibet.

Mantric phrases will also be used by those in the room and, if possible, by the dying person him- or herself. It is recommended that the Sacred Word be chanted in an undertone or on a particular key to which the dying patient can respond. It's also suggested that the top of the head be pointed towards the East and that the feet and hands be crossed. Sandalwood only should be burned in the room and no incense of any other kind permitted, for sandalwood is the incense of the first or destroyer ray that aids the transition into death.[43]

* * * * *

Suicide

Misunderstandings about death are particularly tragic when we come to a consideration of suicide. The psychological stress of contemporary life often leaves people with an inability to manage the chaos they feel within their own heads and that is mirrored all around them in the world. When people lack any sense of meaning in life, when they sense a spiritual aridity, when the crises confronting them seem to lack a solution, the thought of death is sometimes viewed as a welcome relief. And the throwaway society in which we live extends to the discarding of the very gift of life itself.

There is little understanding of the consequences of suicide. If these consequences were better understood, and if spiritual alternatives were embraced, it is unlikely that people would choose this path. According to spiritual teachings, it is just as harmful to the intentions of the soul to take one's own life as it is to take the life of another. It is the soul's responsibility to decide the timing of release from physical form and suicide interferes with that responsibility and a karmic liability is incurred. Suicide, however understandable, is not an option for the alleviation of suffering. It provides no solution or relief from life's problems and in fact only compounds them. While it is true that the physical body no longer suffers after death, the emotional and mental anguish continue unabated, for those bodies still exist for a time after the release from the physical plane life. At the point of death the individual finds himself catapulted into an astral realm that is said to be even more imprisoning than the tortuous physical plane conditions that led to the taking of that drastic step.

Suicide victims need our prayers and our compassion. Holding the soul in the light can aid the victims and their loved ones during this difficult time. It would seem that an understanding of the Law of Rebirth, however rudimentary, could help people who may be contemplating suicide; this is why this teaching is such an essential first step upon the path of spiritual understanding. When people understand the spiritual law and that relief is not to be found via this route, they may be less inclined to take this drastic step.

* * * * *

This teaching on the Law of Rebirth and the new attitudes towards death will be central to the message that the new teacher comes to bring. Many people today understand that this teaching was also a central part of Christ's teaching two thousand years ago but was expunged from the *New Testament* in subsequent centuries by the Catholic Church. The teaching on rebirth will do much to clarify and deepen humanity's understanding of the true meaning of life. As this teaching comes to be better understood, so much human pain and suffering will cease to exist. The whole intent of the path will come to be understood as a means of release and liberation from the trammels of this physical plane. Through a deeper understanding of life we'll come to realize that we are accountable for our actions and that there are essentially no secrets, either from others or from ourselves. Our sense of responsibility to others will deepen as a consequence, and we will all be kinder and gentler with one another.

An expanded understanding of death qualifies the Hierarchy and its actions—in ways that some spiritual seekers may find difficult to accept. The Hierarchy, for example, is not a pacifist organization. This is not to say that its members are pro-war or that they do not take a stand against the blatant injustice and senseless loss of life that characterize most wars, but their expanded sense of consciousness gives them the wisdom to know that sometimes death and destruction are necessary to the fulfillment of the Plan, especially during transition periods.

The Hierarchy, for example, was not in agreement with the pacifist organizations that formed during the first and second World Wars. Loss of life in sacrifice to a higher cause is a noble action and is sometimes necessary. They know that death involves only an apparent separation and that it is indeed part of the soul's plan. But it would seem that humanity today is reaching the point in its evolutionary development where wars and weaponry should be reserved for use by an independent, international peace-keeping force under the auspices of a body such as the United Nations. War will eventually become obsolete. In the interim, no one country should be permitted to be the policeman of the world, dictating to other countries how they should and should not act.

CHAPTER 4

THE SEVEN RAY ENERGIES

THE RAYS DEFINED

The teaching on the seven rays is one of the "new truths" that will come to characterize the incoming age, providing a deepened understanding of many aspects of life. The seven ray streams of vibrantly colored cosmic energy are the very vibrations within matter, space and form that define and infuse all objects, all beings and all events in manifestation. Emanating from great and distant stars within the Great Bear, they pour into and filter through the different constellations, into our sun and the planets within our solar system, and finally into all life forms. The influence of the rays conditions planets, nations and individuals, as well as the animal, vegetable and mineral kingdoms. They give to all things their particular colorings and vibratory notes, their unique qualities as well as their similarities. The ray teaching gives us an energy picture of creation and of life at all levels of being. It provides a means of explaining the intricate interrelationships of all things, spiritual and material; and it proclaims their oneness and interconnectedness.

Broadly speaking, the following is a brief listing of the rays:

Ray One: The energy of Will, Purpose or Power. It is the essence of power, energy and direction. It is characterized by intensity, dynamism and quickness.

Ray Two: The energy of Love-Wisdom, called frequently the Love of God. It is the ray of sensitivity and intuition. This is the great teaching ray.

Ray Three: The energy of Active Intelligence, called the Mind of God. This is the ray of the pursuit of truth, with the intent of manifestation.

Ray Four: The energy of Harmony through Conflict. It is the ray of extremes, of the hill-and-valley experience. This ray stimulates creativity, discrimination and rapid mental perceptions.

Ray Five: The energy of Concrete Knowledge or Science, so potent at this time.

Ray Six: The energy of Devotion or Idealism, producing the current ideologies.

Ray Seven: The energy of Ceremonial Order, producing the new forms of civilization. This ray energy expresses the blending between spirit and matter.[44]

Or expressed another way:
- Ray I — Force — Energy — Action — The Occultist.
- Ray II — Consciousness — Expansion — Initiation — The true Psychic.
- Ray III — Adaptation — Development — Evolution — The Magician.
- Ray IV — Vibration — Response — Expression — The Artist.
- Ray V — Mentation — Knowledge — Science — The Scientist.
- Ray VI — Devotion — Abstraction — Idealism — The Devotee.
- Ray VII — Incantation — Magic — Ritual — The Ritualist.[45]

The psychological application of the ray hypothesis is of particular interest because it provides a practical energy framework for understanding the make-up of individuals and groups. The rays of a person, when determined, studied and understood, will provide that individual, or his counselors or therapists, with a powerful tool for spiritual growth. In certain ways the teaching on the rays is similar to the systems of classification first popularized by the Greek physicians Hippocrates and Galen and later applied by the philosopher Kant. In more recent times similar systems have been popularized by such thinkers as Rudolf Steiner, Carl Jung and George Gurdjieff.

The teaching on the seven rays differs from these previous systems because it is based on scientific principles that will eventually be subject to corroboration and verification as the mechanisms for the measuring of vibratory rates are perfected and etheric vision is developed. These developments are in the process of unfolding now, assuring the rays a central place in future psychological investigation. The rays could be viewed as forming two wide groupings—the odd and even ray lines of force. The odd-numbered rays, one, three and seven (ray five has its own special category), are related more to the form aspect and to physical things. This ray line is "positive" or initiating and masculine in orientation, speaking from the standpoint of polarity. Rays two, four and six, the even rays, are more related to the inner life as it works out through the vehicle of the form. This ray line is more abstract in nature and is concerned with spiritual expression. It is "negative" or receptive and feminine in its polarity.

The ray system of categorization is more complex than the above listed systems of classification in that each individual is a "mixture" of five ray energies, as well as also being subject to the energies that are brought into play via the horoscope. Seven primary energies combine to give each one of us our predominant coloring and quality: the ray of the soul, the ray of the personality, and the ray influences that condition the mental, emotional and physical bodies as well as the powerful influences that emanate from the sun and rising signs. There is also a monadic ray energy which comes into expression at an advanced stage of spiritual development but which sometimes can be sensed and called upon at times of individual and planetary crisis. There are certain rules in ray analysis that generally apply, but not always. Since this science is only in the process of unfolding, we have to remain fluid and open-minded in our approach to this fascinating area of study.

The rays of the personality vehicles can change from one incarnation to the next, helping to round out and enrich the soul's experience, as each ray has its particular strengths and weaknesses that need to be assimilated from life to life. The ray influence at the level of the soul generally remains the same, although at some point in the path those individuals whose soul ray is on the line of attribute (rays four, five, six or seven) will shift to one of the rays of aspect (rays one, two or three). This shift would appear to be in place well before the taking of the third initiation. It is often found that the influence of the personality ray from a previous incarnation (sometimes called a legacy ray) can exert a strong influence in the present life, and this influence can sometimes cause some confusion in the process of ray analysis.[46] The goal of evolution is the gradual blending and "usurpation" of the lower ray energies of the personality vehicles by the ray of the soul.

At the particular stage of development at which many seekers find themselves we are strongly colored by the personality ray. In our youth, when we are in process of "appropriating" our vehicles, the lower energies hold sway, making it difficult to get a clear vision of our own rays. The rays only begin to shine forth as we begin to become integrated, under the influence of our soul and the ray of our mental vehicle. The soul ray shines forth particularly in our service work, where we can draw upon its strength. It is the combination of the soul and personality rays that overwhelmingly make us who and what we essentially are. It is this combination of energies that often brings people together who vibrate to the same influence—the same "color," so to speak. The relationships that are particularly harmonious are those between people who respond to the same personality and soul rays—then we find a lasting friendship or a successful and happy marriage.[47] But these relationships, while comfortable on one level, may lack that learning opportunity that comes through association with others along a different line. Individuals who vibrate to the same soul ray are united at a level of understanding that is ashramic in nature. These relationships defy rational explanation and, no matter what the outer hindrances, withstand the test of time and space and grow in strength from life to life.

Today we find that the ray energy qualifying the mind is also a powerful conditioning factor in the ray make-up of many people because humanity is increasingly becoming polarized on that level. Generally speaking, the mental body is found on either ray one, four or five, although a ray three mental body is also quite common. The Buddha had a sixth ray mind, which the Tibetan described as "a very rare phenomenon."[48] As our minds become lighted, that ray energy begins to shine forth and color us to a powerful degree. Often, a similar mental ray energy will draw people together on service projects; they think alike and consequently understand and can cooperate well with each other. Often, once a determination as to the mental ray is achieved, one can more easily place the other rays.

The emotional or astral body is another potent influence in our lives, often causing the most problems both for individuals and for groups. This vehicle is most often colored by rays two and six, although a first ray astral body can be found frequently in individuals who are taking up the spiritual path in seriousness. The energy of the emotional body is fluid, like water, and is easily stirred up by our reactions to life's events and to other people, and by factors within the environment. That is why we are all asked to "deal drastically" with the emotional vehicle and, as far as possible, transmute its influence in our lives, making it a vehicle through which the energies of divine love and creative inspiration can flow. The physical vehicle is generally found on rays three and seven, although a first ray physical vehicle is not uncommon.

THE SEVEN RAY TYPES

The following description of the different ray types is taken in part from Alice Bailey's book *Esoteric Psychology, Vol. I.* While it primarily describes the conditioning energy of the soul ray, it is also descriptive of the energy of the personality, which can often appear quite similar. It is easy to confuse the two, mistaking the energy of the soul for that of the personality or vice versa. In addition, if there is a "double" influence of a certain ray energy conditioning at the level of the personality, mental, astral or physical bodies, this can bring that ray coloring strongly to the fore in the life expression. And, as mentioned, the ray of the mental vehicle conditions us powerfully; for example, the Christ, who had a second ray soul and a sixth ray personality, nonetheless carried a strong first ray influence through the energy controlling his mental vehicle, which was that of the first ray.

The First Ray of Will or Power

First ray individuals are given the opportunity to work with the energy of the spiritual will. As the Tibetan wrote, "It is a noble task, my brothers, to be channels for the will of God." [49] Such people always possess strong will power, for either good or evil. People on this ray line will always "come to the front" in their field or profession, as they are born leaders. They are people to trust and lean on, defenders of the weak and downtrodden, working to combat oppression and injustice. They are fearless in their approach to all things and utterly indifferent to comment. In those individuals in whom the love aspect is absent, this ray type can produce individuals of extreme cruelty and hardness of nature.

Examples of first ray individuals would be Blavatsky, Napoleon and Churchill. The Western world forever owes a debt of gratitude to Mr. Churchill for his courage and vision that did so much to bring the Nazi threat to the attention of the world when others were faltering and hesitant. Napoleon was a combination of rays one and four, which surely contributed to his utter fearlessness and the inspiration and confidence he inspired in his troops.

The Second Ray of Love-Wisdom

This is the ray of those who pursue wisdom and truth in order to share it with others as their means of service. It is the ray of the spiritual teacher, such as the Buddha (who worked along the wisdom aspect of this ray) and the Christ (who embodied the aspect of love). The Tibetan teacher said of this ray, "The student on this ray is ever unsatisfied with his highest attainments; no matter how great his knowledge, his mind is still fixed on the unknown, the beyond, and on the heights as yet unscaled."

Second ray people possess sensitivity and are often good counselors (in a broad sense of the term), having an understanding of people and a sympathetic response to their difficulties. Their keynote is love, and as this quality develops they can become a magnetic center of lighted energy within their environment. On the lower turn of the spiral, individuals on this ray can easily fall prey to self-pity and dependency. They can be overly attached to the reactions of others, to what they may do or say. It is said that one of the major lessons for the second ray soul is that of detachment, whereas the first ray type often needs to cultivate a measure of "attachment," in the sense of a developed ability to bring about a greater facility of outer expression. The first ray type finds outer displays so distasteful that he can often find himself severely misunderstood because of the perceived hardness of his character.

The shortcoming of the individual who finds himself upon the wisdom aspect of the second ray is to dwell in the ivory tower, within the protection and security of his books and his abstractions, turning a deaf ear to the cry of humanity. If such an individual does not share his wisdom with others, he can fall prey to selfishness that is his particular line of least resistance. Then the mind overtakes the buoyancy of the heart and the individual lives an unfortunate life, or many lives, as the case may be. The second ray type finds his strength through the expression and giving of himself to others. An example of second ray individuals would be the Tibetan himself, Alice Bailey and the XIVth Dalai Lama.

The Third Ray of Higher Mind

The Tibetan says of the third ray individual,

> This is the ray of the abstract thinker, of the philosopher and the metaphysician, of the man who delights in the higher mathematics but who, unless modified by some practical ray, would hardly be troubled to keep his accounts accurately. His imaginative faculty will be highly developed, i.e., he can by the power of his imagination grasp the essence of a truth; his idealism will often be strong; he is a dreamer and a theorist, and from his wide views and great caution he sees every side of a question equally clearly.

The world is indebted to the intellectual achievements of individuals along the third ray line. Their depth of knowledge and intellectual understanding has done so much to shape our world. Many third ray individuals also work in finance and as economists, often turning their attention to civic concerns and humanitarian pursuits. Many writers have a strong third ray emphasis, and we're told that in combination with the fifth ray we find a master of the pen. Contemporary third ray figures might be author Ken Wilber and economist Jeffrey Sachs, architect of the Millennium Development Goals.

The Fourth Ray of Harmony through Conflict

This ray has been characterized as the "ray of struggle." Of this struggle the Tibetan teacher wrote,

> Tamas [the inertia aspect] induces love of ease and pleasure, a hatred of causing pain amounting to moral cowardice, indolence, procrastination, a desire to let things be, to rest, and to take no thought of the morrow. Rajas [the activity aspect] is fiery, impatient, ever urging to action. These contrasting forces in the nature make life one perpetual warfare and unrest for the fourth ray man; the friction and the experience gained thereby may produce very rapid evolution, but the man may as easily become a ne'er-do-well as a hero.

Fourth ray men (and women) "love a tune" and musicians often have the fourth ray strong in their makeup. Fourth ray souls are not active at this time because this ray is not in manifestation, but there are many fourth ray personalities; they work to bring in the energies of the new age, for this type of person is skilled at bridging the past with the future, the old with the new. Shakespeare's Hamlet, the indecisive and long-suffering poet prince, was an archetypal fourth ray figure. A contemporary fourth ray type might be the poet and musician Bob Dylan.

The Fifth Ray of Lower Mind

The individual upon this ray line

> will possess keen intellect, great accuracy in detail, and will make unwearied efforts to trace the smallest fact to its source, and to verify every theory. He will generally be extremely truthful, full of lucid explanation of facts, though sometimes pedantic and wearisome from his insistence on trivial and unnecessary verbal minutiae. He will be orderly, punctual, business-like, disliking to receive favours or flattery.[50]

It is this ray energy, along with that of the seventh ray, that conditions scientific inquiry. The clear impersonality of this mentally polarized ray energy has contributed so much to the world through the pursuit of truth in such fields as science and philosophy. Many of the world's physicists have been on the cutting edge of bridging the subtle and the material worlds. They are believers in the true sense of the word—for their beliefs are devoid of sentiment and attained through a penetration into the inner dimensions of reality. In many ways, they provide the model for group work.

The Sixth Ray of Devotion

This is called the ray of devotion. In its "higher" manifestation, the sixth ray individual is characterized by an intense pursuit of truth and, when working in a "lower," more destructive fashion, by fanaticism in its many guises. The Tibetan characterized this individual in the following manner:

> Everything, in his eyes, is either perfect or intolerable; his friends are angels, his enemies are very much the reverse; his view, in both cases, is formed not on the intrinsic merits of either class, but on the way the persons appeal to him, or on the sympathy or lack of sympathy which they shew to his favorite idols, whether these be concrete or abstract, for he is full of devotion, it may be to a person, or it may be to a cause.[51]

Two powerful examples of workers upon this ray would be Paramahansa Yogananda and Martin Luther King, Jr.

The Seventh Ray of Ceremonial Order or Magic

This is the ray of the individual who delights in all things done decently and in order. An individual along this ray would make a brilliant general, a fine sculptor, a financier, an architect, a choreographer or a priest. That is not to say that all people working in those professions belong to the seventh ray but rather that its influence would often characterize the type of work done in those fields. Along with the second ray, the seventh ray is the ray energy most concerned with healing. As this ray comes into prominence in the world, we are witnessing an explosion of interest in alternative healing modalities as well as advances in medical research technologies.

The seventh ray has also provided the impulse behind the revolution in communications technology. The energy of the seventh ray facilitates the "spiritualization" of substance and the seventh ray individual knows how to work lovingly with this golden lighted substance. A strong seventh ray in one's ray makeup makes an individual highly organized, a "master of detail," and able to handle justly and fairly the responsibilities that are entrusted to him. Such a person can realize his or her goals upon the physical plane and does so in an orderly and efficient fashion. Examples of seventh ray individuals would be Marie and Pierre Curie and George Balanchine.

* * * * *

An understanding of the rays is generally a matter of intuitive perception that unfolds gradually over time. Sometimes we find that by being in someone's presence we can tune into his or her energies and the rays reveal themselves to us. We can also learn about the rays from other people who have somewhat mastered this science and are willing to share their perceptions with us. They can help us to understand the subtleties of ray analysis and how to pinpoint characteristics that qualify a certain ray energy working through a certain vehicle. Of course, none of this is an exact science as yet, and we cannot know with certainty whether or not our conclusions are correct. When approaching the subject of the rays, it is important to keep an open mind and think for ourselves. But sometimes it is also true that other people can help us see the rays with greater objectivity and detachment, and it is the course of wisdom to take their perceptions into consideration. Over time, as our understanding deepens, we may have to reevaluate our earlier conclusions.

Much can be learned about the rays through a study of the Tibetan's books, particularly *Discipleship in the New Age, Vols. I & II* (in which he gives the five conditioning ray energies for each individual in his group, accompanied by a series of letters that help us to understand the psychology of the individuals involved) and the five-volume series of *A Treatise on the Seven Rays* and *The Destiny of the Nations*. The rays should not be viewed with a cookbook mentality. As essential as it is for us to gain a semblance of understanding of ray analysis, it is important to keep in mind that we are all shaped by many factors—the rays, astrological influences, the powerful ray conditioning that comes through the country of our birth and our genetic heritage, and by our evolutionary status, previous incarnations and karmic assets and liabilities—to name a few. All of these factors combine to color each of us.

One of the easiest ways to begin a study of the rays is through a consideration of the rays of the nations as given out in *The Destiny of the Nations*. In this way we come to understand the rays through the lens of nations and their people and the broad strokes that color them. We all hold a picture in our minds of the Russian temperament and how it differs from the French or the Italian. As we study the ray colorings of the different nations and people of the world, we can learn much. The nations each possess a soul and a personality ray, as do the cities of the world, and as we reflect upon these qualities, our understanding grows.

As mentioned, astrological factors also play a strong part in "coloring" us, and that is why the volume *Esoteric Astrology* is included in the teaching on the rays. Astrology is said to be the "greatest and oldest of all the sciences," one that must be restored to its original beauty and truth, thereby revealing the Plan.[52] The teaching on esoteric astrology involves a new method of interpretation that is unfolding at this time. From the esoteric perspective, the energy of the rising sign is related to the soul's destiny in any particular incarnation and its ray; the sun sign reveals the nature of the present incarnation and the secret of the personality ray; and the moon sign indicates the past and the liabilities we carry with us from previous incarnations. Esoteric astrological analysis is an exceedingly complex and powerfully synthetic science. We're told, for example, that a Master can take one look at an esoteric astrological chart and attain a crystal clear perception of the exact rate of evolutionary development of the individual under consideration.

A study of the rays and astrology will help psychologists in the future to come to a deeper understanding of human nature. As yet, however, this science is still in its infancy, and it will take the concerted effort of those individuals who are willing to experiment with this information in order to bring it more into the mainstream of psychological investigation. As the conditioning ray energies come to be better understood, psychologists will be able to work more effectively. Instead of focusing solely on past traumas and childhood conditioning, they will begin to work scientifically with the power of the soul that can more effectively heal cleavages and bring the personality into alignment with its higher destiny. Meditation techniques utilizing sound and color in accordance with the different ray types, applied by those who possess spiritual insight, can do much to aid in the process of integration. Integration between soul and personality is the key, the *raison d'etre*, of the entire field of spiritual or esoteric psychology.

CHAPTER 5

GLAMOUR AND THE SEVEN RAYS

No glamour, no illusion can long hold the man who has set himself the task of treading the razor-edged Path which leads through the wilderness, through the thick-set forest, through the deep waters of sorrow and distress, through the valley of sacrifice and over the mountains of vision to the gate of Deliverance. He may travel sometimes in the dark (and the illusion of darkness is very real); he may travel sometimes in a light so dazzling and bewildering that he can scarcely see the way ahead; he may know what it is to falter on the Path, and to drop under the fatigue of service and of strife; he may be temporarily sidetracked and wander down the by-paths of ambition, of self-interest and of material enchantment, but the lapse will be but brief. Nothing in heaven or hell, on earth or elsewhere can prevent the progress of the man who has awakened to the illusion, who has glimpsed the reality beyond the glamour of the astral plane, and who has heard, even if only once, the clarion call of his own soul.

Alice Bailey, *A Treatise on White Magic*

THE PLANETARY CONDITION OF GLAMOUR

We all face many challenges on the path of development, some within ourselves (conditioned by our particular ray combination) and others seemingly presented by our environment. It is helpful to remember that on the path nothing is hidden and at each turn we must face ourselves.[53] The wise individual, therefore, sees the world as in a mirror.

As we travel this path of self-realization, we are continually confronted with situations that appear to conspire to hold us back and trap us on the "wheel of rebirth." These obstacles take many and varied forms and can serve as springboards for growth if we learn from them. In the Ageless Wisdom teachings our shortcomings, our blind spots, are called glamours, conditions that veil and hide the light.

The Tibetan defines glamour as "a bewildering, deceiving and illusory energy-form which seeks to sidetrack and mislead the neophyte and which is attracted to him by ancient habit and old controls."[54] Each one of us is subject to many forms of glamour that are the result of different factors. These glamours impede our ability to see clearly. Until we overcome these ancient controls, we will live and work from a state of limited potential. The process of dissipating glamour is a progressive development; as its more overt forms are eradicated, we become subject to its increasingly subtle manifestations.

At this time our planet is suffering under the weight of the most negative condition of glamour of all time. It is a definite, substantial thing. The entire planet is covered with what could be described as a thick layer of astral mist and fog that is composed of all the unredeemed qualities of human nature—the separateness, selfishness and material desires that characterize the lower aspects of physical plane living. The nature of this fog is said to be of a nature so dense and thick that it practically impedes life itself. Yet within this negative condition humanity lives and moves—seeing all of life from a skewed and distorted perspective.

It is no wonder then that life is so difficult today and that so many people are suffering and losing their way, for we are literally blinded by present conditions. Most of us are so accustomed to this negative situation, so encased within the veils of this world and the confines of our limited perceptions, that we do not even realize how powerfully it is affecting us.[55] Fortunately, many people are beginning to awaken to the situation and are beginning to see things more clearly. The changes that are presently taking place upon our planet will lead eventually to a drastic improvement in this condition so that future generations will not have to live under its dominance and will, consequently, live freer and happier lives.

Each ray type is subject to particular glamours, or limitations.

Ray One

Weaknesses: self-centeredness, ambition, the Messiah complex in the field of politics, aloneness, pride, aloofness, and the enforcing of one's will upon other and groups.

Qualities to be acquired: tenderness, humility, sympathy, tolerance, patience.

Ray Two

Weaknesses: the love of being loved, the Messiah complex in the field of religion, a too-complete understanding that negates right actions, self-pity, fear, undue sensitivity and selfish service.

Qualities to be acquired: love, compassion, unselfishness, energy.

Ray Three

Weaknesses: manipulation, criticism, scheming, coldness, inaccuracy in details, absent-mindedness.

Qualities to be acquired: sympathy, tolerance, devotion, accuracy, common-sense.

Ray Four

Weaknesses: a love of harmony aimed at personal comfort, a desire for peace at any price, self-centeredness, worrying, vague artistic perception, strong passions, lack of moral courage.

Qualities to be acquired: serenity, confidence, self-control, purity, accuracy.

Ray Five

Weaknesses: pride, criticism, arrogance, over-assurance based on a narrow point of view.

Qualities to be acquired: devotion, sympathy, love, wide-mindedness.

Ray Six

Weaknesses: devotion, attachment, idealism, jealousy, over-rapid conclusions, fiery anger, personal loyalty, sentimentality.

Qualities to be acquired: strength, self-sacrifice, purity, truth, tolerance.

Ray Seven

Weaknesses: sex magic, bigotry, pride, narrowness, vanity and superficial judgments.

Virtues to be acquired: wide-mindedness, tolerance, humility, gentleness and love.[56]

As we build in the virtues through the use of the "as if" technique, we will find ourselves coming more powerfully under the conditioning energy of our soul ray. Through lack of attention, our weaknesses will begin to recede into the background of our consciousness.

Types of Glamour

What follows is a brief listing of some of the more obvious obstacles to spiritual growth that sometimes face seekers on all the seven rays:

Desire

The incessant desire to possess and to grasp at that which we do not have has been one of the most powerful driving forces in human evolution. For this men and women have lived, loved, and often died. It has led to untold suffering and despair as people have repeatedly sacrificed their highest and noblest intentions—their very humanity—to satisfy the insidious web of desire. We all know much about desire, for we have all desired many things.

Sometimes it is desire that spurs us into action and provides a catalyst for change, but it cannot bring lasting happiness, for it is based upon ephemeral things. The Buddha taught the limitations of a life mired in desire and the means to overcome it. We in the West are, perhaps, finally ready to hear his message, as evidenced by the popularity of Buddhist teachings. Although we have so much, we also know that material goods cannot bring us lasting happiness. Buddha taught that desire was the root of all suffering and that as we give up desire for the things of the world, we will gradually begin to find the happiness we seek.

The basic message of the Buddha was contained within what have come to be called the Four Noble Truths. These Truths hold that:

1. Existence in the phenomenal universe is inseparable from suffering and from sorrow.
2. The primary cause of suffering is desire for existence in the world of phenomena.
3. Cessation of suffering is brought about by eradicating all desire for existence in this universe of phenomena.
4. The way to the cessation of suffering is by treading the noble Eight-fold Path, wherein are expressed right belief, right intentions, right speech, right actions, right living, right endeavor, right-mindedness and right concentration.[57]

Perhaps these Noble Truths seem a hard road to follow, sapping the joy out of existence. They may appear too exacting and too serious, and demand too many sacrifices from us. But this reaction would be a misperception of the Buddha's essential message, for this is a compassionate path, a path of loving-kindness, as demonstrated so well by His Holiness the XIVth Dalai Lama. The tremendous outpouring of interest in Buddhism in the West demonstrates that this teaching has found a deep chord of resonance within many seekers today, which is a reflection of the depth of spiritual hunger alive in the world. The following of the Noble Truths and the Eightfold Path acts as spurs for us to seek and find happiness in a higher and deeper source, one based on the pursuit of more lasting truths.

The Buddha taught the uses of the mind to bridge the gap between the unreal and the Real through the state of union that is yoga, the yoke that holds all things together. He forged the antahkarana out of the substance of himself and brought down light from heaven. He became a conductor of electricity by taking himself in hand and through skillful means cut away the egotism that caused the energy to be short-circuited. The Buddha destroyed the artificial barriers that hold us to the past and pressed ahead into the eternal Now. He did this, he said, by remembering a childhood experience of pure joy that came upon him spontaneously while playing alone under a flowering rose-apple tree. He remembered the effortless sense of bliss that arose at that time when he was free, open and innocent. In turn he used that remembrance to free himself in the Now and went on to teach the way of release from suffering and bondage to all those who chose to follow in his footsteps and brought about the enlightenment of many in his day. He was not content with doctrines and formulas that didn't work and strove, within himself—depending upon himself alone—to tread the way that brought release.

Fear

> Will you not, with determination and because the world cries out for help, cast away fear and go forward with joy and courage into the future?
>
> Alice Bailey, *Esoteric Psychology, Vol. I*

Fear is another quality that hinders many people. It is so pervasive that there are few who do not suffer from it in one form or another, but, perhaps because it is so prevalent and so close to us, we become blind to the many ways that it hinders us. We fear so many things—failure, success, sickness, old age, change, love, loss of love, sex, self-expression, and many conditions related to our families, especially our children. Yet when we succumb to fear, we limit our ability to live and love freely; we pull down a curtain between ourselves and life and act in ways that are contrary to our higher self.

The inability to master fear is one of the main factors holding back many individuals from taking a major step forward in their spiritual development. It is helpful, therefore, to observe ourselves closely, to uncover and face our fears. Alice Bailey counseled people to do what their inner voice guided them to do, even if it meant losing friends in the process. She was a brave woman, yet she also had many fears—and many friends!

The qualities to be cultivated in the astral body that will lead to the lessening of fear are the obvious—calm, stillness, serenity and quietude. What is not so obvious is the means of achieving these states. The Tibetan told us that we could conquer fear by the following actions:

- By a constant watching of all desire, motives and wishes and by emphasizing those of a high order.
- By a constant daily attempt to contact the higher Self and to reflect his wishes in the daily life.
- By definite periods daily directed towards stilling the emotional body.[58]

This glamour powerfully conditions individuals found upon the second ray line of energy.

Pride and Related Conditions

Other problems, related to mental development, are pride and criticism. These conditions spoil the service that we could be rendering. As mentioned, it is the pride of intellect, so strong within the Western world, which has resulted in the present condition in which the mind has become the slayer of our better, or higher, self. Alice Bailey said that she had a strong recollection of having been very prideful in a previous incarnation and that she had learned a valuable lesson as a result of the experience that enabled her to achieve relative freedom from this condition, a rare thing to find. She said that the example of the Masters should keep us all humble, for in comparison with their achievements, anything that we could possibly do is really quite insignificant.

The cultivation of humility and the *Gita*'s counsel on the "relinquishment of gain" are antidotes for these conditions, for they give us a truer perspective about ourselves and our circumstances. The Tibetan counsels that humility has no relation to an inferiority complex but instead to a realistic and balanced view of oneself based on fact, on vision and on time pressures: the *fact* of the Hierarchy (which puts all human achievement in perspective); a vision of the Plan and the part we and our co-workers can play in it; and the recognition that in this time of emergency we have to work fluidly, with the ever present need to "modify, qualify and adapt" our work. These qualities will result in an "adjusted sense of right proportion,"[59] enabling us to see life and its events with the requisite dispassion.

The cultivation of humility by individuals with much first ray in their equipment would enable them to work more effectively in service of the Plan.

Spiritual Self-Interest

Another problem today is the manifest self-interest of many spiritual seekers. This takes many and varied forms but could broadly be described as a quality that leads people to place service to the self above service to humanity. This route leads to a cul-de-sac from which it is difficult to escape and produces a type of spiritual myopia. Too many people today find that there is always another class to take, retreat to attend, special diet to pursue, or guru to visit—the list becomes endless. And while these activities can be very helpful in many respects, too often they become the primary focus of interest, leaving little time for anything else as the individual becomes wrapped up in him- or herself.

The importance of the physical body lies in its refinement, which leads, paradoxically, to the ability to transcend it by making it a vehicle through which the energies of the higher self can flow. Many people and groups today are doing much to facilitate this refinement through attention to exercise, diet, and the myriad alternative healing modalities that are blossoming throughout the world. The cultivation of healthier physical bodies is an important aspect of spiritual training. But the body needs only enough attention to keep it in good working order, leaving us free to do other things.

The Goal

> I told you that a time comes when the initiate knows that the astral plane no longer exists. For ever it has vanished and has gone. But when the initiate has freed himself from the realm of delusion, of fog, of mist and of glamour, and stands in the clear, cold light of the buddhic or intuitional plane, he arrives at a great and basic realization. He knows that he must return to the 'seas' which he has left behind, and there dissipate the glamour. But he works now from 'the air above and in the full light of day.' No longer does he struggle in the waves or sink immersed in the deep waters. Above the sea he hovers within the ocean of light, and pours that light into the depths. He carries thus the waters to the desert and the light divine into the world of fog.
>
> Alice Bailey, *The Rays and Initiations*

Whatever our status on the path, we all have limitations that hold us back from a deeper penetration into the light. One of the tasks of every teacher, be it our soul or a more advanced individual who has us in his or her charge, is to help reveal to us the nature of our particular glamours or "blind spots," qualities that we usually refuse to recognize and consequently project onto others. One of the difficulties of human nature is our seeming inability to face and give attention to these unredeemed aspects of ourselves. We all have blindness in certain areas of our lives; we all have faults, limitations, inertia and darkness. If we continually retreat in self-defense when life and circumstances attempt to get through to us, we will remain encased within ourselves and lose the opportunity that is being offered to us to move forward on the path. If, on the other hand, we live under the cloud of a constant self-depreciation, overly concerned with the little self, we will also lose sight of the bigger picture.

What the teachers who stand before us ask is that we look at life and situations from a deeper perspective. We're asked to be ready for unexpected discoveries about ourselves and others. As the Tibetan wrote, "One of the first lessons which a disciple needs to learn is that where he thinks he is strongest and where he finds the most satisfaction is very frequently the point of greatest danger and of weakness. Astral conditions are oft seen reversed; hence the glamour which often overcomes a disciple."[60]

The fact that many spiritual seekers at least admit to the existence of glamour in their lives is a big step upon the way. Most people do not have any such recognition and instead "deify their glamours and regard their illusions as their prized and hard won possessions."[61] Any success that we have in freeing ourselves from glamour clears the way for those who follow after, and makes their path easier. This is the Great Service.

There are specific spiritual techniques given out by the Tibetan that can be used by individuals and groups to aid in the task of dissipating glamour. They are contained in the final section of his book, *Glamour: a World Problem.*

CHAPTER 6

THE TRANSFER OF RAY ENERGIES

THE RAYS AND THE WORLD

The rays, as mentioned, condition all forms of life, not merely the human. Great and powerful ray influences ceaselessly cycle in and out of manifestation, conditioning our world for hundreds of years at a time. The Ageless Wisdom gives information about the rays controlling the different civilizations, and we can learn much from this study of the esoteric history of our planet. But perhaps the most important thing we can attempt to understand about the rays is the powerful shift that is now occurring. At any given period there are always a number of different ray influences conditioning all forms of life, but generally there is one major ray energy controlling. Today we are moving from a civilization ruled by the sixth ray into one conditioned by the seventh.

The Outgoing of the Sixth Ray of Devotion or Idealism

Under the influence of the outgoing Piscean age, the energy of the sixth ray, the ray of devotion or idealism, has been the predominant energy in manifestation. This ray began to pass out of manifestation in the year 1625, yet it still remains the most powerful conditioning factor in the world today, and many people are heavily under its influence.[62] The rays cycle in and out of manifestation over the course of hundreds of years.

Over the course of its manifestation the quality of a ray energy changes. As the energy begins to wane in influence and reaches the end of its long cycle of manifestation, its qualities begin to crystallize, causing the negative aspects within its manifested forms and conditioning attitudes to become more apparent. At the same time that one ray influence is crystallizing and passing out of manifestation, another, newer ray influence is coming in. This adds to the tension in the world, particularly when the ray energies are changing at the same time that the zodiacal ages are changing, as is the case today. This situation is creating a "polarization" as some people cleave to the influence of the past and others respond more readily to the new, incoming energies. This creates the basic "battleground" between the conservative and the progressive types that we see in the world today.

One of the highest expressions of sixth ray energy is the religious impulse. It was this influence that helped spread the religious teachings of the Buddha, the Christ and Mohammed during its cycle of influence. It stimulated humanity's aspiration towards truth and spiritual liberation. But now, as this influence begins to wane, we see its lower manifestations, which we call fundamentalism, taking hold of many aspects of life.

The fundamentalist problem extends beyond the physical threat of terrorism to include entrenched attitudes at the emotional level. The fanatical aspect of the waning sixth ray influence manifests particularly through those individuals or nations whose individual psychology is powerfully conditioned by the sixth ray. It is important to keep in mind that we are only given ray information for a few countries. Some of the countries that are influenced by the energy of the sixth ray are the United States, Russia, Italy and Spain (although it should be kept in mind that the sixth ray rules the U.S. and Russia at the level of the personality while Italy and Spain have sixth ray souls).[63] At times, this sixth ray influence can lead to a type of blind idealism and an ingrained tendency to try to enforce their views on others.

It becomes clear when studying the rays just how closely the higher and lower manifestations of any particular ray energy resemble one another. This makes it difficult to see events clearly during this time of the crystallization of the energies. Often false truths—or half truths—can be presented in such a manner that people can easily be taken in by the seemingly noble rhetoric. This was particularly apparent in Germany during the rise of Fascism, as it is today within the Christian and Muslim fundamentalist movements.

The Incoming Seventh Ray of Ceremonial Magic

At this time there is a new ray influence that is coming into manifestation, the seventh Ray of Ceremonial Order. This ray began cycling into existence in 1675.[64] Its energy blends exceptionally well with the incoming energies of Aquarius, and this combination will result in the widespread illumination of consciousness.[65] The seventh ray is attuned to the energy of the physical plane, to matter, and it will result in many changes in the forms of our civilization and the increased ability to "bring through" and embody spiritual impression in physical creation. In the passing Piscean age, consciousness was turned away from form, and the physical body and the so-called "material world" were rejected and considered as impediments to spiritual development. This mindset and the resulting sense of "sin" created many difficulties for people. This repression of many natural human reactions led to the present swing to the other extreme. We currently find ourselves in a society in which the form and the material aspects of life are being raised to new heights. Out of this swinging between the poles, an eventual balance will be reached.

The incoming seventh ray brings many individuals into incarnation who are strongly conditioned by this influence—mostly at the soul, personality, and/or the physical level. They are the pioneers who are shaping the new age with its new forms and new ideas. The seventh ray creates the place where "the highest and the lowest meet." A blending and merging of spirit and matter can occur with a consequent inpouring of the spiritual Will directly into humanity, creating synthesis and a sense of wholeness in the world.

Under the influence of the sixth ray, the approach to the spiritual path was mystical and reverential, concerned primarily with devotion to the teacher. The approach to spirituality will change dramatically under the influence of the seventh ray and will take on what might be described as a more "scientific" coloring. The mystic works primarily with the energies of the heart, whereas the new type of spiritual workers will seek to blend the energy of the heart with that of the mind, resulting in a more proactive type of spirituality.

In the past, spirituality was divorced from the world and there was a tendency for spiritual seekers to retreat in order to undertake their practice. Today there is a growing understanding by many people that the spiritual path must be realized within the world, often within the cities, the "jungles of the West," where it will change and adapt to meet the different needs and levels of consciousness of people today. It is the Western seeker who will eventually perfect the practice of raja yoga—an oral teaching that was transcribed thousands of years ago by a great Indian teacher by the name of Patanjali. These raja yoga techniques are known as the "kingly science of the mind" through which the brain of the practitioner can become illumined by the energy of the soul. Raja yoga techniques include, at the same time that they supersede, all other forms of yoga.

The transfer of ray energies at the present time is particularly difficult because of the chakras, or energy centers, involved. Each ray energy works out through and stimulates a particular center within the body. In the case of the sixth ray, the energy works through and stimulates the solar plexus center, the center that is linked specifically to the emotional nature. This is a very powerful center within humanity, and its stimulation is one of the reasons why the world is in such a state of crisis, with strong desires and emotions manifesting on all sides. The seventh ray is linked with the sacral chakra, the center that is related to sexuality. This is one of the reasons why human sexuality is being so stimulated at the present time. The whole planet is caught up in a crisis of stimulation in these two most primal areas of life, creating a very difficult dynamic.[66] The solution to the present problems can only begin to work out as humanity learns to use the mind to clarify and dispel the powerful energies that control us at the physical and emotional level.

CHAPTER 7

MONEY:
THE CRUX OF THE PROBLEM

WHY WE ARE HERE
for the World Trade Organization Summit, Seattle 1999

Because the world we had imagined, the one
we had always counted on, is disappearing.
Because the sun has become cancerous
and the planet is getting hotter.
Because children are starving in the shadows
of yachts and economic summits.
Because there are already too many planes in the sky.

This is the manufactured world
you have come to codify and expedite.
We have come to tell you
there is something else we want to buy.

What we want, money no longer recognizes
like the vitality of nature, the integrity of work.
We don't want cheaper wood, we want living trees.
We don't want engineered fruit, we want to see and smell
the food growing in our own neighborhoods.

We are here because a voice inside us,
a memory in our blood, tells us

you are not just a trade body, you are the blind tip
of a dark wave which has forgotten its source.
We are here to defend and honor
what is real, natural, human and basic
against this rising tide of greed.

We are here by the insistence of spirit and the authority of nature.
If you doubt for one minute the power of truth
or the primacy of nature
try not breathing for that length of time.

Now you know the pressure of our desire.
We are not here to tinker with your laws.
We are here to change you from the inside out.
This is not a political protest.
It is an uprising of the soul.

Anonymous

TOWARDS A SUSTAINABLE WORLD

This anonymous plea, born of the anguish of a moment and the experience of a lifetime, reflects the concerns of many people who recognize the enormity of the challenge and opportunity that stands before us at this time. The success of our efforts to build a sustainable future will define not only the immediate years ahead but generations to come. Our failure will lead irrevocably to the continued dominance of those who work with shortsighted and selfish aims and to our eventual destruction. Now is the time to move beyond the endless debates over issues of relative un-importance (tactics used to delay and distort), and towards the implementation of those measures for which all men and women of goodwill long, and upon which our survival depends. We, the peoples of the world, have reached the point where we can no longer wait for our leaders and our governments to tip the scales of the present delicate balance. Too much time has already elapsed. It is time for the people of the world, through the collective strength of an enlightened public opinion, to hold leaders accountable and to realize our vision for a better world.

Because of the growing complexity of global events it is important that we stay informed and engaged, while continuing to cultivate the necessary detachment, harmlessness and essential simplicity that have been the defining qualities and contributions of seekers throughout time. The Tibetan urged us to cultivate peace in turmoil, power in fatigue, and persistence in spite of bad health.[67] He said that often our progress will be made in spite of, and not because of, existing conditions. We are called to keep our fingers upon the planetary pulse in the recognition that only by this means can we become the arbiters of the change and redirection that we seek.

The most pressing problem at this time is the gross economic imbalance which lies at the root of all the others. The issue of economic sharing and redistribution—is *the* issue, as its impact extends to all other areas of life. The right distribution of the money energy of the world is essentially the crux of the problem in relationship to the change and reconstruction work that is needed in all areas of life upon our planet. In a certain sense, this would appear to be such a simple problem to resolve, yet in actuality it remains anything but. Recent economic trends have led to a widening of the gulf between rich and poor, both within and between countries.

We live in a world in which 2.5 billion people live on under $2/day; one billion have no access to clean water; one-third of the global population lives without electricity; 30,000 children die each day from poverty and another 30,000 from preventable diseases—totaling 22 million needless deaths each year. The positive result of this situation is that it has spawned the growing movement for sustainable development and many other initiatives. While progressive growth has been made in the developing world, large numbers of people still live in extreme poverty at the same time that the developed nations continue to spend one trillion dollars annually for armaments production and half of the one hundred wealthiest entities in the world are corporations.

The aim of the growing movement for sustainable development is to improve the lives of all people everywhere without consuming the earth's resources beyond their replenishing rate, by balancing the global free market and assuring increased access to communications technology between peoples and nations. People have been gathering together in working sessions and protest marches in the attempt to voice their concerns and to demand change. They are working to define and articulate a new set of values that includes democracy, environmental sustainability, social equity, human rights, cultural and biological diversity, and right livelihood. This work is related to the exceedingly complex problems such as labor relations, outsourcing and immigration. The individuals working in this area are attempting to resolve the problems by moving beyond self-interest to the interests of the common good. We are living in an age in which new dynamics are needed, a time when many people are recognizing that they are indeed global or planetary citizens, and pledging allegiance to the good of the whole in the firm recognition that this will ultimately work out to the benefit of all the parts. The old paradigms of the individual nation-state, invoking its right to unilateral action, must cede to a higher, collective authority.

The wisdom teachings predict that we are approaching the time when there will occur a vast restructuring of the entire worldwide economic order through the intervention of a group of highly powerful individuals who will come forward to reorient the present unequal distribution of the world's resources—moving them under the control of an international body that will ensure their equitable distribution. This group is taking shape at this time.

Money for Spiritual Work

The greatest hindrance to the realization of the spiritual work also lies in the lack of money with which to carry it out. The money exists, we all know that, yet the problem remains how to redirect it towards spiritual purposes. The growing impulse of Aquarian energies will lead to the eventual free and full circulation of the money energy of the world, but in this interim period it is still often in short supply. The Ageless Wisdom teaches that all forms of life are intertwined and connected through a vast web of relationship. Essentially, there is no separation, no mine and thine. Yet our attitudes towards money have frequently kept humanity separated and divided, leaving large segments of the planet both literally and figuratively in the dark.

Viewed from the spiritual angle, money is understood as a concretized form of energy—a golden, "lighted" substance that is increasingly becoming a fluid, "liquid" substance. This change is having profound implications for us all. As money moves out from underneath the weight of its former crystallized state, it is being freed to flow in new directions in alignment with its higher spiritual destiny as "the consolidation of the loving, living energy of divinity." In this regard we're told in the teachings that "the greater the realization and expression of love, the freer will be the inflow of that which is needed to carry forward the work."[68] Traditionally money has been used for individual and family need and for the satisfying of our selfish desire; as we enter the Aquarian Age, it is beginning to be used for group and world need and as an instrument of goodwill and right human relations.

We live in a world in which tremendous amounts of money are wasted on nonessential and luxury items while millions die of starvation and many others are starving for spiritual truth. If even a fraction of the money in the world were redirected towards meeting humanity's material and spiritual needs, it could do so much to help ameliorate the present conditions.

Money is, in a certain sense, the lifeblood of any project, and without it the work atrophies and dies. However, a great campaign to raise money is not necessary; the focus instead should be placed upon the dissemination of ideas. Money flows into avenues that are magnetic and vibrant, into ideas that carry authenticity and that consequently evoke a ready response from people's minds and hearts. Concepts taken from the Ageless Wisdom teachings, while of ancient origin, are still largely unknown among the general public, and money is needed to disseminate them more widely among the masses of humanity. People are hungry for something to believe in, to feel a sense of hope and expectancy for the future. The task then becomes one of devising a means of presenting the ideas in such a way that people will understand and respond to them.

Traditionally, part of the problem in funding spiritual work has been that some spiritual seekers have turned their interests so wholly away from physical plane matters that money and the means of managing it barely make their list of priorities or interests. This creates a problem because this seeming "otherworldliness," this lack of interest in the practical affairs, often renders them unable to attract the needed money with which to carry forward their work. So many negative attitudes towards money have developed over the centuries and hampered the work that needs to be done at this most crucial time in our planetary history. A valuable exercise, therefore, is to begin to examine our attitudes and our personal sense of responsibility in relationship to the money that flows through our hands, with the intent of beginning to see clearly the ways in which we are contributing to the present conditions.

Humanity's relationship with money is changing under the influence of the incoming energy of the seventh ray. A new breed of spiritual worker is emerging: individuals who know how to work effectively upon the physical plane, with all the skills and resources that more worldly people and organizations use to market their wares, dedicating them instead to spiritual purposes. Eventually, under the full tide of the Aquarian impulse, there will be a blending of spirit and matter and a free and full circulation of the money energy of the world. And there are spiritual techniques that can facilitate this process. They involve the use of the spiritual will by groups of individuals who are living sacrificial lives, asking noth-

ing for the separated self and giving all they can to the work that
needs to be done. By such means they will create a channel through
which the needed supply will be directed. It is the combination of
need, the ardent desire to meet that need, and the sure knowledge
that it can be met that will release the needed funding for the
building of the new world. We work with an understanding of
the law of supply and demand—establishing the right conditions
within consciousness that create a magnetic aura around the work,
which in turn attracts the "supply" needed to carry out the work
to be done.

* * * *

"We must all live simply that others may simply live."

CHAPTER 8

TOWARDS A NEW MANNER OF RELATIONSHIP

> Love, for many people, for the majority indeed, is not really love but a mixture of the desire to love and the desire to be loved, plus a willingness to do anything to show and evoke this sentiment, and consequently to be more comfortable in one's own interior life. The selfishness of the people who are desirous of being unselfish is great.
>
> Alice Bailey, *Glamour, A World Problem*

> In the vale of illusion the symbol oft engrosses attention and that which it represents is forgotten.
>
> Alice Bailey, *A Treatise on White Magic*

It is only natural that during this period of planetary energy transfer, all forms of life are being disrupted, including the forms of our relationships. Distortions in this area of living always occur when a civilization is crumbling and the old order is giving way to the new. So it is today as we pass through this period of the "withering of the Law."

Because intimate relationships often stir up the physical and emotional bodies, they can easily pull us out of alignment with our higher self, thereby contributing to the overall condition of glamour in our world. As Aquarian energies pour into our planet, they are producing an opening of the heart and an urge towards universal love. But unfortunately these energies are often distorted and travestied as they pour into our largely material world, and they sometimes work out in a rampant and indiscriminate sexuality. As mentioned, humanity's desire nature is also being stimulated by the incoming seventh ray energy, which works through the sacral center, the center most closely related to sexuality.

As with many aspects of life today, sexual expression has exploded to such an extent that it seems as if we are living in a world gone mad, caught up in the throes of desire and constantly seeking new and more exciting ways of satisfying that desire. Sex is not the way to enlightenment, even if our misguided culture seems to make it appear so. The present situation has led to disease, unwanted children, pain, sorrow, and much hardship for many people. But no one, it seems, knows how to turn things around and bring about a more measured response to this problem.

In a certain sense, this powerful expression of human sexuality could be seen as a reaction against the repression and inhibitions of the past, when sex and the body were considered evil and sinful—attitudes that often colored perceptions of women as well. It's understandable, therefore, that we are now moving in the opposite direction. Eventually we will find the middle way of balance governing this important aspect of our lives as conditions within the planet settle down, producing a greater measure of calm and stability.[69]

For hundreds of years, the monastic tradition provided a means by which many people were able to follow a spiritual path in relative freedom from the cares and worries of everyday existence. For women, in particular, the opportunities offered by the monastic life in terms of education and freedom from poverty and the dangers of childbirth were understandably viewed quite favorably. Now we live in a different world, a secular age in which celibacy does not necessarily serve the purposes of the day. It is not helpful for seekers to shut themselves away, without any possibility of expression for their natural instincts. The vows of celibacy demanded in certain religious traditions have created unrealistic expectations and have led to the abuse of innocent people. Addressing this issue is part of the necessary housecleaning needed within the world's religions prior to the return of the World Teacher.

The spiritual path could, however, be viewed as a higher understanding of the celibate life. As the Tibetan wrote, "The celibacy required is that of the higher nature to the demands of the lower, and the refusal of the spiritual man to be dominated by the personality and the demands of the flesh."[70] Sometimes spiritual seekers do have to demonstrate the developed capacity to stand alone. But this enforced or chosen path is often said to be the result of past excesses that need to be adjusted in the present life or cycle. Celibacy is not, therefore, necessarily a sign of high spiritual status.[71]

As we impose a discipline and a rhythm upon our lives, we will find it easier to undertake the rigors that serious spiritual work entails. People talk openly about the need for the "conservation of energy" in regard to the ecological crisis presently afflicting the planet. But there is an equally pressing need for the conservation of energy in our individual lives. The body is most assuredly a delicate ecosystem, and we are wise to treat it with the same care and concern that we would like to see extended to the planet. The powerful energy that fuels human sexuality if mishandled can easily pull us out of alignment with our higher self. But it's not always easy to control. Many great spiritual seekers throughout time have struggled with their sexuality—the Buddha, Jesus, St. Francis, St. Paul, Gandhi, Helen Keller, Martin Luther King, Jr., and others. The overstimulation that results from uncontrolled sexual energy has led to the downfall of many sincere people.

The Ageless Wisdom teachings indicate that the present problems related to sex can and will be solved in the coming decades. This will involve a shift in attitude. Eventually we will come to see that much that is thought of as progressive in the way of sexual activity is in fact the remnants of a distant past that would best be left behind. The Master Djwhal Khul has said that a solution to the problem of sex will involve a concerted, collective effort—one that calls upon the wisdom and counsel of many minds, many teachers and yogis.[72] Great yogis know the power found in the conservation of energy, and in the future this knowledge will be more deeply understood. The time is not far off when people will develop etheric vision that will allow them to understand more fully than they do today the consequences of their actions, because they will see the effect within the activity of their chakras. This will result in many changes in behavior.

As the new age unfolds, we will evolve new forms of relating to each other that will be the natural outcome of our living more integrated, soul-infused lives, and this will release a tremendous amount of creative energy. But in the interim, as the old forms crystallize and break apart and the new forms have yet to evolve, there is much pain and suffering in the process of liberation. Perhaps what we are doing is redefining what it means to love—refashioning the experience along more equitable, Aquarian lines. The soul desires nothing, hopes nothing, asks nothing for the separated self. As we begin to approximate this expanded conception of love, we will experience a lessening of the present distressing conditions. Soul relationships are founded on love, not attachment; they enable us to leave others free to grow and develop according to the wisdom of their own soul, not as we want them to. Cyril Scott's *Initiate* series presents a model of relationship that could perhaps be viewed as a forerunner of the Aquarian age.

We are not expected to be alone upon our journey, at least not all the time. Even the Masters and initiates of high degree enter into the marriage relationship. It is, after all, perhaps the most valuable field of life experience and potential service, for the sharing of life's joys and sorrows teaches us many things. The spiritual path demands a measure of solitude; through solitude, the "rose of the soul flourishes"[73] and the connection with the inner worlds unfolds. Solitude is, therefore, often the rule for many people treading the path—yet solitude can be found or created within a healthy relationship when each party is free to have time and space, independent of the partner.

We are moving into the age of the group, into a condition of collective consciousness, and this reorientation will have profound implications for the marriage relationship. The increasingly collective nature of life will lead to a lessening of the pressure on couples to fulfill each other's needs. Individuals will be brought together for a larger purpose than their individual happiness. The service provided by couples could be the creating and raising of children, but increasingly people will come together to undertake specific work, in relationship with their discipleship responsibilities.

The young people coming into incarnation have evolved a different perspective about relationships. They have observed much disruption in relationships over the course of their short lives and this has had a powerful effect, making them wise beyond their years, with positive and negative consequences. Up until the past century, most marriages were short-lived, due to early death of one or both spouses; marriages were also disrupted by long periods of separation on account of war or economic concerns. Now that people are living longer, perhaps it is unrealistic to think that couples can always adhere to the "until death do us part" injunction contained within the marriage vows. People change and grow throughout the course of their lives, and not always in the same direction or at the same pace. It is sometimes the course of wisdom to sever ties rather than maintain a relationship that has outlived its usefulness.

Marriages that achieve the ideal—uniting two people on the physical, emotional and mental planes—are rare today. We might find, for example, that the physical body of one person is involved in the relationship while the physical body of the other is not, but there may be an emotional attraction and connection. Sometimes the mental body is involved and activated but the physical and emotional bodies are left out. When the involvement is found on all three levels, you find that rare instance of a true union and a resultant happy marriage.[74] When there is this ideal merging of all three planes of involvement, the right conditions exist in which souls can be provided with the appropriate forms in which to incarnate.

The incoming seventh ray is called "the marriage ritual of the Son," and under this influence there will be stricter marriage laws in order to provide greater protection from the natural impulsiveness that so often characterizes romantic love. The changes will not result in making it more difficult to end a marriage, but it will become more difficult to enter into the arrangement. Hasty marriages and marriages among juveniles will not be permitted.[75] Young people will be taught and counseled before they undertake this important step in their lives.

So while today many people enter rather blindly and foolishly into marriage, the future will see a more "scientific" or business-like approach to the whole arrangement. In a certain sense we will find ourselves moving into a new type of "arranged" marriage, on a higher turn of the spiral. The prospective partners will be studied from the angle of the potential suitability of their union along the lines of their ray and astrological qualities as well as their relative evolutionary development. A consideration of these factors, and of heredity, will contribute towards the making of more enlightened choices. And, as a consequence, it seems likely that the incidence of divorce will drop. And those who do face divorce will surely find the whole process less painful, as they will be functioning with greater detachment. As we grow in soul alignment, we come to trust the soul's wisdom, knowing that the law works, even in the midst of change and disruption in this delicate area of our lives.

The freedom inherent in a good relationship is based upon trust and respect. Relationships that are secure in their love are expansive, leaving both partners free to include many other people within their sphere of influence. As people learn to relate to each other increasingly as soul-infused personalities, there will be a general deepening, and a real spiritual connection will become possible. Friendship between the sexes will become the foundation upon which this change will come about, and we can see this happening today. People will also be much more likely to sacrifice their personal wants in favor of the greater good of their relationship and the family of which they are a part.

We will eventually reach a point where the true expression of love between the sexes will be transferred to a higher plane of consciousness. True love will manifest through the spoken word, and not as readily through physical plane expression as it does now. It is interesting to explore the strong correlation between creativity and sex. Many artists, for example, have a strongly developed sexual expression that highlights the relationship between the sacral center and the throat center. In the years to come, as sexual energy begins to be transmuted and lifted to the throat, this will work out in an incredible flowering of human creativity, leading to new forms of art, poetry, music and philosophy.[76] This creative expression will increase dramatically after the year 2025 when the fourth ray comes into expression again.[77]

As we struggle and fight our way into a greater measure of light through the overcoming of our glamours, we eventually find ourselves entering into the freedom to be who and what we essentially are—beings capable of ever-widening and deepening manifestations of ceaseless and boundless love. Love is not really a personality expression but rather a spontaneous outflow of mind and heart that embraces all it encounters. When we love truly, freed from the grasping of the separated self, we are released from so much of the pain that has for so long affected the human condition.

How we manifest that love in our modern world is part of the transformative process that is underway during this transition period. Love is the goal—in both the personal and the universal sense. And while we're clearly not yet capable of expressing true spiritual love, we are irrevocably moving in that direction. As we traverse this way of compassionate unfoldment—which is the path of the bodhisattva warrior—we find that we need to summon the courage and strength of the inner warrior. This strength frees us to express the love of the bodhisattva without being crushed by the experience or deterred from its undertaking by the seeming obstacles and limitations that abound in our world.

CHAPTER 9

SEEKING THE WAY

Rest not, above all, from your meditation work; keep the inner link; think truth at all times. The need and the opportunity are great and all possible helpers are being called to the forefront of the battle. All can be used in some way, if the true nature of sacrifice is grasped, if skill in action is developed and if work without attachment is the effort of each and all of you.

Alice Bailey, *A Treatise on White Magic*

The Path of Meditation

Meditation is perhaps our most powerful tool for both individual and planetary transformation. It leads to the coordination of our soul, mind and brain, and eventually unites us with our inner group and provides the means by which we can work together in service to humanity and the planet as a whole. Through meditation we "become the path" as we seek the way from within the very fabric of consciousness itself. That path is the golden, gossamer thread that leads us irrevocably "from darkness to light, from the unreal to the real, from death to immortality" and eventually releases us from the endless round of birth and death and onto the path of the higher evolution, which is ever the way of fuller service. Over time, we come to realize that our "sitting for development" has a much larger, universal purpose than our individual development and is in fact part of a vast planetary process. As we meditate, we increasingly find ourselves becoming aligned within the rhythm of the planetary heartbeat.

Sometimes people disparage spiritual seekers, viewing them as self-absorbed, impractical idealists, remote and distant from the concerns and cares of the world and its affairs. And while this attitude clearly does characterize some people, increasing numbers of seekers today recognize the need for an engaged spirituality. For them, there are no distinctions or arbitrary barriers between the spiritual and the so-called material worlds. Their reality is centered in the firm recognition that the whole intent and purpose of a spiritual life is to use our thoughts and actions to align ourselves with the vast and ever-present supply of spiritual energy that can then be turned towards the uplifting of all lives that suffer under the weight of present planetary conditions. It's said that "one disciple thinking truth can revolutionize his [or her] environment," and a group so thinking can change the world. And because of the power wielded by trained spiritual workers, the group does not need to be large in order to be effective in its work.

There are many different kinds of meditation, many different types of yoga. The practice advocated in the wisdom teachings is known as raja yoga, the "kingly science of the mind." Through the raja yoga technique the mind becomes "fixed in intention" and eventually all the lower vehicles are brought into alignment with it and the personality stands within the soul's light. This technique has been preserved down the centuries in the East by the spiritual Hierarchy, within what is called the Trans-Himalayan school. Seekers who follow this path are asked to refrain from other meditative practices so as not to incur difficulties that can arise from the mixing of techniques. All true growth as the result of meditation is naturally slow and progressive, carried forward over the course of many years of quiet practice. Quite often we work in the dark and the inner process of transformation is not always apparent in our waking brain consciousness. But if we do the work, our efforts will eventually bear fruit. Any apparent rapid growth in meditation is the result of disciplines established in previous incarnations.

This path follows the precepts set down by the great Indian teacher Patanjali. His work was a compilation of the oral teachings and practices that had been handed down throughout the centuries in India. Patanjali's *Yoga Sutras* provide the most comprehensive and authoritative manual for the raja yoga technique and stand as a central doctrine in both the Hindu and Buddhist traditions. There was some controversy as to the dates of Patanjali's life and work, but it is generally thought that he lived somewhere between 820 B.C.E. to 300 B.C.E,[78] Some Hindu authorities, however, place him as early as 10,000 B.C.E. His methods can be studied and practiced by many different types of seekers; they have stood the test of time and provide the means of advancement for students on all the many levels of development—from the aspirant first placing his or her feet upon the path all the way up to and including the great initiates and the adepts. The bedrock of the raja yoga technique is ever the heart of the development that precedes it. The spiritual person whose heart is open and expressing love and service is laying the foundation for this path. Patanjali outlined the basic qualities that we all need to build into our lives in the Commandments—"harmlessness, truth to all beings, abstention from theft, from incontinence and from avarice" and in the Rules—"internal and external purification, contentment, fiery aspiration, spiritual reading and devotion to Ishvara (or the inner teacher)." The Commandments and Rules become our sure guidelines upon the path.

The Ageless Wisdom teachings stress that different meditation forms are needed for Eastern and Western students due to the fact that our bodies are differently constituted. In fact, it's said that Eastern meditation techniques could prove dangerous to certain types of Western students. In the past, because of the long tradition of spirituality, vegetarianism and the proximity of the Masters that existed in the East, people's bodies were naturally more refined and better suited to the rigors and strains that long periods of meditation place upon the lower vehicles. The Tibetan sought to bring forward meditative forms that were better suited to Western students who work amidst the coarseness of the vibrations that exist in the West. Generally these forms are shorter and more dynamic in nature. Long periods of meditation, the premature use of breathing exercises, and any other practices that are used to force a rising of the kundalini energy are strictly to be avoided by new students. Meditation brings in fiery energies and we must take care to watch for any signs of possible overstimulation as a result of this practice.

In past centuries, the meditative life was largely undertaken within the monastic traditions, often in solitude, by withdrawing from worldly concerns and following a path of spiritual retreat. Today this is changing as spiritual practices flood into the West with many "lay" people incorporating meditation into their daily lives. In many respects it is much more difficult to undertake a spiritual practice amidst all the challenges of contemporary life. At this time when the dharma comes to the West, we are learning the more difficult task of holding the focus amidst the fury of outer events in the recognition that the place of retreat must be found within ourselves, and not so much in outer circumstances.

The practice begins with the period of alignment by the stabilizing and calming of the physical, emotional and mental bodies. The use of the sacred word, the OM, sounded either audibly or inaudibly, aids in this process. Often, especially in the beginning, the attainment of mental focus is difficult, but we begin by centering ourselves within the ajna center, withdrawing our consciousness deep within ourselves. Eventually the soul begins to "grip" the vehicles, enabling facility of concentration and a positive orientation. In a certain sense, our approach to the practice of meditation is no different from the training undertaken by any individual who begins a new area of study—be it academic, artistic or vocational. We learn over time to work more effectively, and we are aided in this process by the lineage and example of the many teachers who have paved the way for us.

The raja yoga technique incorporates work with a seed thought, an aphorism, quality, or symbol, that when pondered in the process

of meditation becomes a vehicle for the expansion of consciousness. Alice Bailey described meditation with seed as similar to the
process of preparing a lecture: the mind gathers facts that are used
to penetrate into the deeper layers of thought that, in turn, reveal
the quality behind the outer form. Visualization is a central aspect
of the raja yoga technique; this is understood not so much as the
picturing of images but rather as a means of learning to wield and
direct energy in conformity with the purposes of the soul.

Fanaticism is not called for in the meditative life. As we read in
the *Bhagavad Gita*, "There is no meditation for the man who eats
too little or for the man who eats too much, or for him whose habit
it is to sleep too much or too little. But for him who is regulated
in food, in work, regulated also in sleep and in waking, meditation becomes the destroyer of all suffering."[79] The first step on the
meditative path is implementing the rhythm of the daily practice.
It is easy to say that we do not have time to meditate. But if we
take our spiritual life seriously, we will come to view meditation
as our most essential and vital tool and we will make the time for
it. Establishing this practice does, however, demand discipline and
perseverance, the ability to keep on keeping on, even when conditions conspire to interrupt the rhythm. It is important to have a
quiet space and time without interruption to meditate. It is best
to draw as little attention to yourself as possible. In this way your
practice can be viewed more or less as a normal activity, not one
that arouses suspicion and hostility among your family members
and friends. At first it is recommended that the meditation period
last from fifteen to twenty minutes. This is a considerably shorter
period than that advocated by many other techniques practiced
at this time. With time and experience, and as the lower vehicles
become accustomed to the new vibrations, the practice can be
extended.

It is best to meditate in the morning, as the mind is freer at
that time from the busyness and concerns of the day. There are
special energy currents that accompany the early morning hours,
and these can be tapped by the meditator and used to set the tone

for the day. But if one's schedule does not permit a morning meditation, it can be undertaken at some other time

Eventually meditation becomes a way of life, not only a practice we undertake each morning. It establishes a spiritual intention, and we go through our day with its radiatory and magnetic effects conditioning all aspects of our lives. Meditation can help develop new qualities—increased efficiency, perseverance, a one-pointedness in our manner of living, organizational power, an ability to eliminate the nonessential, and a greater facility in overcoming challenges. By raising our consciousness into the head and by attempting to govern our lives from that point, we can significantly subdue the emotional nature. We all come to the practice of meditation with different attributes, and some people are naturally better suited to the practice than others. But whether we find the practice natural or taxing, it stretches us to reach into new and expanded areas of consciousness and works out in an increased capacity to serve the Plan.

An ancient fable compared the practice of meditation to the act of dyeing a piece of cloth a bright yellow color and then leaving it to dry in the noonday sun. Eventually the color in the cloth will fade, but if during the next day it is re-dyed and left again in the sun to dry, it will not fade as much. As this process is repeated daily, the cloth will retain more and more of its color with each passing day until it no longer fades at all and retains its yellow brilliance at all times. So, too, is the path to enlightenment a process of "dyeing" our consciousness on a daily basis.

The path is not merely a figure of speech but refers to an actual condition created by "weaving" within the threads of consciousness itself. In the wisdom teachings this path is known by its Sanskrit name, *antahkarana,* the rainbow bridge. Collectively, we are building a vast bridge within consciousness that possesses all the many colors of the rainbow to which students on all the different colored rays contribute. We can be encouraged in this building work by the recognition that many individuals throughout time have followed this way and found release—we follow after them just as we, in turn, are carving out the path for those who follow us.[80]

Meditation has been compared to the breath, for it conforms to this natural and universal rhythm of the inbreathing and out-breathing of energy. All of life is part of the cyclic ebb and flow of spiritual energy. As we begin to submit our lives to these cycles, we come to vibrate synchronously within the rhythm of this larger whole of which we are an infinitesimal yet vital part. Meditation is essentially a means of centering ourselves so that we can contact, hold and distribute spiritual energy. At the present time most of us are learning these techniques in accordance with our ray type and personality conditioning. But we are rapidly moving into that time when teachers will come forward, primarily within the new schools of initiation, who will be capable of working effectively with their individual students to provide a type of "customized" meditation format. These meditations will meet the different needs of the students in their charge according to their particular ray and astrological conditioning. These teachers will possess the ability to see more fully into their students' consciousness and, through this sensitivity, develop those forms and those spiritual techniques that will accelerate their students' progress on the path. They will, in effect, assume a role similar to that which the Tibetan undertook with the students in his charge as outlined in the *Discipleship in the New Age* books. Until that time, however, we can work with the existing forms available and adapt them, as we are able, according to our needs.

Even though meditation is generally undertaken alone, it helps to always hold in mind the essential group nature of this practice. Meditation is the means by which we come to recognize the fact of our group and the realization that as we unite with that group our capabilities for true service are exponentially magnified. Towards that end, we can begin each meditation period by linking up in consciousness with our group brothers and sisters. Many people also find the use of a mantram to be helpful to make the connection more real. If we establish the discipline and follow the meditative instructions as given out to us, over time we can expect surprising and lasting results that will work out in many changes in our lives and our environment.

The following thoughts from the Tibetan may bring a measure of understanding of the objective that stands before us at this time:

> Radiance we are and power. We stand forever with our hands stretched out, linking the heavens and the earth, the inner world of meaning and the subtle world of glamour.

> We reach into the Light and bring it down to meet the need. We reach into the silent Place and bring from thence the gift of understanding. Thus with the light we work and turn the darkness into day.[81]

MANIFESTING THE VISION: THE PATH OF SERVICE

> Those who are not ready for the coming events will be blinded by the emerging light and bewildered by the revealing wonder; they will be swept by the living breath of God, and it is to you that we look to fit them for the event.
>
> Alice Bailey, *Esoteric Psychology, Vol. 1*

All sincere efforts at spiritual development have as their aim the steadily increasing ability to bring through or release our essential nature in some form of service to others. This service work is the most important part of the spiritual path and the means of giving back a fraction of what has been given to us. Service is a law, and it is the primary idea to be grasped at this time, for it opens us wide to the incoming tide of energies from Aquarius,[82] the sign of the Water Bearer, pouring forth the water of life. And while people talk about service and are eager to serve, there are many misconceptions about it, so it is important to attempt to come to a deeper understanding of just what service is. It is a subtler concept than is generally understood, and we often interpret it too concretely and thereby fail to understand its finer implications.

Service is the natural expression of the soul, and by aligning ourselves with the soul we cannot help but serve.[83] Service releases us from our separated selves and our problems, which doesn't mean those problems go away, but we learn to live with them so that they no longer interfere to such an alarming extent as they once did. We can ask our soul to direct our steps and trust that our needs will be taken care of. We can ask to be of fuller service and have faith that we have been heard, and opportunities will open up that will make this possible.

It is helpful to remember that often what our soul attempts to convey to us may run counter to the comfort and rhythms of our personality self, and we should be prepared for this. It is not easy to upset the "establishment"—the established rhythms and structures within our individual lives or the established structures within groups and society at large. That is why all who travel this route, this "forcing process" that is the path of spiritual return, must call upon the courage of their souls.[84]

There are of course many avenues for service. That's why we must choose wisely before we take up a path of service. We can seek out our motives and ask ourselves why we make the choices we make. It is important to understand that there are relatively few people to do the spiritual work of the world, whereas there are many more people who are better equipped than we to work in the more established, traditional forms of outer service. Perhaps this is why the Tibetan teacher said that one of the primary impediments to the reappearance of the world teacher lies in the inertia of the average spiritually-minded man and woman.[85] There are so many distractions, so many nonessential things to occupy our time and attention that too often little or no energy is left for the things that really matter.

The things we value so highly about ourselves are generally not the things that are viewed as being of most importance from the perspective of our soul. Since most of us are still largely living within the confines of the material world, we tend to place a more material interpretation upon our lives and our service work. In this way, we err by putting the cart before the horse. Someone once said that people who have had near-death experiences report that when they passed through the portal of death they came to realize that the only thing that matters in life is the amount of love that we have expressed and shared with others. That's it.

The external aspects of service therefore diminish in importance as we learn to serve in a more subjective fashion—silently, behind the scenes, and with our group. Gradually we develop the capacity to "stand, not only in spiritual being, but together with others, working with them subjectively, telepathically, and synthetically."[86] We learn that it is not the outer achievements that matter—our job or outer service projects, our creative work, the force of our words and our personalities. What matters is something else, something subtle, less tangible, that happens largely within the silence of our own hearts and minds, related instead to the group aspect of our lives and work. When we place the emphasis upon the soul, upon the inner recognitions, we learn to work and follow in the footsteps of the great servers whose lives and work stand as models to us all.

There are currents of energy that become available to us, especially as we learn to work with groups and feel ourselves to be part of a vast and intricate pattern of relationships.

The Tibetan gave us guidance in this subjective work from an ancient "Book of Rules." He wrote,

> All true esoteric schools begin with the control of the astral body and, the chela had to memorise and practice these three rules after he had made some real growth in the manifestation of harmlessness.

> Rule I. Enter thy brother's heart and see his woe. Then speak. Let the words spoken convey to him the potent force he needs to loose his chains. Yet loose them not thyself. Thine is the work to speak with understanding. The force received by him will aid him in his work.

Rule II. Enter thy brother's mind and read his thoughts, but only when thy thoughts are pure. Then think. Let the thoughts thus created enter thy brother's mind and blend with his. Yet keep detached thyself, for none have the right to sway a brother's mind. The only right there is, will make him say: "He loves. He standeth by. He knows. He thinks with me and I am strong to do the right." Learn thus to speak. Learn thus to think.

Rule III. Blend with thy brother's soul and know him as he is. Only upon the plane of soul can this be done. Elsewhere the blending feeds the fuel of his lower life. Then focus on the plan. Thus will he see the part that he and you and all men play. Thus will he enter into life and know the work accomplished.

A note, appended to these three rules says:

These three energies—of speech, of thought, and of purpose—when wielded with understanding by the chela and blended with the awakening forces of his brother whom he seeks to aid, are the three energies with which all adepts work.

It is almost impossible to translate these ancient formulas into adequate terms, but the above rough paraphrase will convey the idea to the illumined; these rules sum up the few thoughts which the average aspirant needs to grasp about the right direction of energy, and for which he is ready.[87]

THE GREAT INVOCATION

I challenge you to penetrate, through meditation, more deeply into the vital meaning of these words, these amazing words. They embody, as far as is possible in modern language, a formula which has been in possession of the Hierarchy ever since it was founded on Earth, but which is only now available for use, owing to the point in evolution reached by mankind. The wonder of these mantric stanzas is that they are comprehensible to members of the human family and to members of the Kingdom of God. They mean one thing to the ordinary man, and that meaning is good, powerful and useful; they mean another thing to the man upon the Probationary Path, for he attaches to the words a deeper and more esoteric meaning than is possible to the man who is entirely polarized in his lower nature; these words mean still another thing to the disciple affiliated with and functioning consciously in an Ashram; to initiates and to the senior Members of the Hierarchy, they convey a still higher and more inclusive significance.

Alice Bailey, *Discipleship in the New Age, Vol. II*

The Great Invocation (original wording)

From the point of Light within the Mind of God
Let light stream forth into the minds of men.
Let Light descend on Earth.

From the point of Love within the Heart of God
Let love stream forth into the hearts of men.
May Christ return to Earth.

From the centre where the Will of God is known
Let purpose guide the little wills of men—
The purpose which the Masters know and serve.

From the centre which we call the race of men
Let the Plan of Love and Light work out
And may it seal the door where evil dwells.

Let Light and Love and Power restore the Plan on Earth.

The Great Invocation (adapted wording)

From the point of Light within the Mind of God
Let light stream forth into human minds.
Let Light descend on Earth.

From the point of Love within the Heart of God
Let love stream forth into human hearts.
May the Coming One return to Earth.

From the centre where the Will of God is known
Let purpose guide all little human wills—
The purpose which the Masters know and serve.

From the centre which we call the human race
Let the Plan of Love and Light work out
And may it seal the door where evil dwells.

Let Light and Love and Power restore the Plan on Earth.

When the World Teacher decided to return to outer manifestation, in June 1945, he gave out to humanity an ancient and powerful prayer that has come to be known as the Great Invocation.[88] This Invocation for Power and Light is said to be the most powerful tool we have to help prepare human consciousness for the coming events. Although it was only given out for our use a few decades ago, the Invocation is actually of ancient origin. Its potency is so great, however, that it could not have been given out earlier. The timing of its release had to be right. While many prayers are used with personal intention, the power of the Invocation lies in its *impersonality*; it is not focused upon the needs and wants of the individual but rather on the larger concerns of humanity and the planet as a whole. As such, its use by large numbers of people can produce powerful changes for all forms of life.

No organization, religion or spiritual group "owns" the Invocation. It is a nonsectarian prayer and can be used effectively by all people. Although in its original wording it refers to Christ, it is not a Christian prayer and can be used by people of all faiths and also those who hold to no particular faith at all. The Invocation has currently been translated into over seventy languages and is used in most countries in the world, although it must be more widely distributed before its true potency can be realized. Humanity has never come together and used a single spiritual mantram. We haven't tested the effectiveness of such an activity although certainly the Lord's Prayer holds a central place within the Piscean age. The Great Invocation can hold a similar place of prominence within the coming Aquarian Age.

Over the years many individuals and groups have offered alternate wordings for the Invocation. And while many people naturally prefer to use the Invocation in its original wording, the adaptations have been welcomed by many others. The purity and strength of the original Invocation is such that we are told that not a day goes by in which the Christ himself does not sound it forth.[89] Indeed, Foster Bailey (Alice Bailey's husband and coworker) said that this act of cooperation between Alice Bailey and the Tibetan, in April 1945, was perhaps their single greatest achievement. The Tibetan said that up until their cooperative endeavor, the Invocation had existed in seven ancient word forms. Their painstaking translation, finished as the sun was rising, was said to have left Bailey completely drained yet exhilarated, and to have produced a complete union of her mind with that of the Tibetan. The Invocation is said to constitute the World Teacher's complete new utterance. It is perhaps understandable then that serious students of the Ageless Wisdom teachings might prefer the original wording. Indeed, the adapted wordings were never meant to supplant the original; they are merely intended as alternatives that might appeal to a larger audience during this transition period.

The Invocation was given out over sixty years ago. The world has changed drastically since that time. Over the years, it became apparent that the Great Invocation would only achieve the status of a world prayer (as the Tibetan had foretold), if it was adapted to meet the varied needs of people today. We live in an age in which the use of language is very important in creating unity or divisiveness. Language that is perceived to be archaic or offensive (however pure its original intention) is rejected out of hand by many people today. The growth of the movement for the liberation of women ignited a demand that language reflect an egalitarian worldview, and the original wording of the Great Invocation offends many who hold to those sensibilities.

The Masters are pragmatic individuals; they leave it up to their students to make decisions regarding important matters related to their work in the world. Those who would promote this work cannot afford to ignore the realities of the time and must be willing to "modify, qualify and adapt" their message to the forms in which it can be received most readily in the time in which they live. Failure to change with the times has limited the effectiveness of our most important tool for planetary transformation. And even the Tibetan teacher encouraged slight adaptations in the wording of the Invocation when it was being used with specific groups.[90] And, therefore, those who adhere too vehemently to established traditions, impede the work to be done.

It is, however, important for us to reflect upon the power conveyed through the careful choice of words and their mantric cadence used in the original wording. In the case of the Invocation, many of the objections raised to the original wording relate to the use of the words "men" and "Christ." But as we ponder the inner meaning underlying these words, we come to realize their essential inclusiveness. The word man, for example, comes from the Sanskrit "manas," and means "the one who thinks." As viewed through this lens, sexual stereotypes fade away. As mentioned earlier, "Christ" is the name of an office, the World Teacher, the head of the spiritual Hierarchy, and has no intrinsic relationship to any organized religion. As students reflect upon these deeper considerations it is hoped that when possible, they will choose to use the original wording, thereby enhancing the effectiveness of this most powerful tool for human and planetary transformation.

In the future we can expect that the present barriers in understanding posed by misinterpretations of language will not exist and people will come to appreciate the original wording. But now, during this interim transition period, what matters is that people use the Invocation, because that is the only way by which its power can be released in the world. It is hoped that in the coming years the Invocation will begin to be recognized more widely by the global community.

The Great Invocation is used by members of the Hierarchy with "constancy, exactitude and power,"[91] and the Tibetan encouraged us to use and distribute it. Another important point related to the use of the Invocation should be held in mind. We are advised not to turn the Invocation into a peace prayer. The Tibetan wrote,

> Peace and the love of peace can be a deadening soporific. It is usually selfish in purpose, and people long for peace because they want to be happy. Happiness and peace will come when there are right human relations.[92]

The Tibetan started an activity known as Triangles to foster the effectiveness of the Great Invocation. People who participate in Triangles form part of a worldwide network aimed at the transformation of planetary consciousness. Triangles is a simple meditative and visualization exercise in which three people agree to link up each day to use the Invocation as a form of planetary service. This work is subjective and does not have to be coordinated in time and space. An important aspect of the Triangles work relates to its ability to transform the configuration of the planetary etheric body. At the present time that body is said to be composed of a series of squares that are inert conductors of energy, the square being the symbol of the "lower" personality. The effectiveness of the Triangles network lies in its ability to transform the etheric structure of the planet into a series of interlocking triangles, the symbol of the soul.

CHAPTER 10

MEDITATION AT THE FULL MOON

He who faces the light and stands within its radiance is blinded
to the issues of the world of men; he passes on the Lighted Way to
the great Centre of Absorption. But he who feels the urge to pass
that way, yet loves his brother on the darkened path, revolves upon
the pedestal of light and turns the other way.

He faces towards the dark, and then the seven points of light
within himself transmit the outward streaming light, and lo! the face
of those upon the darkened way receives that light. For them the way
is not so dark. Behind the warriors—twixt the light and dark—blazes
the light of Hierarchy.

Alice Bailey, *Discipleship in the New Age, Vol. II*

AN OPEN DOOR

Throughout time many religious festivals have been held in
conjunction with the full moon. Humanity has intuitively
sensed the beneficence of this time, and the beauty of the moon's
reflected light continues to be a source of fascination and wonder.
And while it is true that spiritual inspiration is available to us at
any time, during the full moon period it is more actively present
because of the alignment that is set up between our planet and
the sun.

The cycle of the full moon is the "power point" of the spiritual
month, and many individuals and groups come together to work

in meditation at this time. The importance of this period is related, ironically, to the fact that the influence of the moon is out of the way. According to the teachings of esoteric astrology the moon is basically a dead shell and symbolizes the past, a type of prison house that should be left behind.[93] When its influence is negated, the full energy of the sun, the symbol of the soul's light, impacts freely and directly upon human consciousness, providing a vivid outer symbol of an inner spiritual experience.

The full moon approach is, in reality, a five-day period—the two preceding days, the day of the full moon itself and the two succeeding days. The two days preceding the day of the full moon are known as days of preparation, when we work to establish an inner alignment with the soul and our group. These are days of "renunciation and detachment" when we prepare spiritually for the actual day of the full moon, which is known as the "day of safeguarding." On this day, and particularly at the exact moment when the moon is full, we simply attempt, as far as possible, to stand in spiritual being—acting as silent channels in alignment with hierarchical intent, focusing our thoughts upon the need of humanity and the planet. The two succeeding days are known as the days of distribution, when the energies contacted are "shed abroad in our hearts, through our group and throughout the world."[94]

At the time of the full moon each month a door stands open between the spiritual Hierarchy and humanity. It is through this open door that inspiration can flow outwardly into human consciousness, facilitating closer contact and a relationship between all those individuals who are receptive and sensitive to the vibration of the inner planes. We are asked to pause and turn our consciousness within, away from the outer concerns and activities of our daily lives and, in a collective group effort, work together in meditation and thought to create a channel (sometimes called the "rainbow bridge") through which spiritual light can flow into human consciousness.

There is a "thinning of the veils" that occurs at this time, and as we develop the tools of inner listening, we can become more sensitive to the impressions from the soul; our lives and our work can come to be guided increasingly from within. The Tibetan teacher asks that we "look for results" during this time. He wrote, "Watch for these experiences—intuitive, telepathic and spiritual."[95]

As more people take up the discipline of the full moon work, we can collectively bring about real changes in the world. The power of a united invocative group, working with selflessness for the good of the planet as a whole, is exceedingly strong. As people are educated as to the importance of this monthly cycle, they will want to cooperate. Enlightened religious and spiritual leaders could work to make this happen. The observation of the monthly full moon cycle is perhaps the most important discipline that we can undertake. By establishing this practice within our lives, not only are we helping the planet by contacting and distributing spiritual energies, but we are also working with a technique that can serve to solidify our group relationships with our coworkers throughout the world. Full moon work expands our hearts, deepens our love and helps to break down the barriers that separate us one from the other.

Each monthly full moon meditation is influenced by the astrological constellation that is ruling during that particular month. Each sign of the zodiac has a key quality, or qualities, that can be built into human consciousness by meditating upon them. For example, the sign of Sagittarius is intended to convey the quality of direction and control, and Scorpio brings in the quality of triumph through struggle, whereas Capricorn is related to the path of initiation. Each sign also has a spiritual keynote that can be used in meditation.

The full moon period is a time for intense meditation and quiet, subjective work. It is a time when we can attempt to make contact with our soul and our spiritual group. As we attune ourselves to this inner rhythm of the full moon work, we will find that we become aware of subtleties we had not noticed previously. No matter where we are, or what we are doing, it is a time when we can each take the opportunity to link up in consciousness with the organized spiritual push that is going on throughout the planet.

For this type of full moon meditation to be effective it is helpful to meditate in group formation as close as possible to the actual time of the full moon, preferably sometime within the preceding eighteen hours.[96] This is when the energies are building and when contact with the inner group is more readily accessible. Prior to beginning meditation, it is suggested that we link up in consciousness with our group brothers and sisters throughout the world—any individuals whom we might know who hold to a spiritual orientation. We can include them within our consciousness and surround them with the energy of light and love. During this time, it is also important to remember those workers who have passed over to the inner side, for they too are working with us, perhaps in a more effective fashion, for they work free from the impediment of the physical body. We can also include coworkers who may have fallen away from the path, for they are still connected with the work upon the inner planes and should not be forgotten.

The fluctuations that occur in the outer group life do not exist upon the inner planes; there we work free from the separative barriers that still often color the outer groups. Upon the inner planes there is union. At the time of the full moon each month we have the opportunity to strengthen and solidify these inner links that can, through time, help to heal and restore harmony upon the physical plane by the subjective support that we can all give to one another. The full moon opportunity can provide us with the means of bringing about healing, enabling us to all go forward within the bonds of light and love—leaving the past behind. Apart from our group work, no matter where we are, we can always observe the exact time of the full moon as an opportunity to link up in consciousness with all the other people throughout the planet who are cooperating with this group work.

THE WESAK FESTIVAL AND THE CHRIST'S FESTIVAL

Just as the full moon period constitutes the high point of spiritual contact during the monthly cycle, the Aries, Taurus and Gemini full moons are the high points within the annual cycle. Each year during these full moon periods sacred and solemn ceremonies are held by the great teachers in a remote region of the Himalayan mountain range. The festival of Wesak, which occurs at the time of the Taurus full moon, is linked with a legend described by Alice Bailey in a booklet distributed by the Lucis Trust:

> [I]n a little valley in Tibet, on the further side of the Himalayas…the earthly ceremony of blessing is supposed to take place, and to that valley many people in and around the district find their way, as pilgrims towards the light. There, at the time of the full moon, a solemn ritual is performed, which can be as definitely seen and heard as can any ceremonial in any of our great cathedrals.

Bailey tells of two dreams, seven years apart, during which she participated in a strange ceremony:

> The events recorded were so clear and vivid, and the details each time so identically the same, that it was impossible to dismiss the dream as an idle fantasy, or to regard it as simply the usual kind of dream phenomenon. It was twenty years later, when I read a description of the Wesak Festival, that I discovered that it was that which I must have seen. My dream apparently indicated a real happening. Several times I have met those who have similarly dreamt, and who have wondered what it was that they then saw. When a dream seems uniformly the same when registered by different people all over the world, when the details of the dream remain unchanged, and when it is found that the dream is based upon a definite ceremonial which did take place at the time, there is surely room for much discussion, for the evocation of a real interest, and perhaps for the evidence of testimony to a fact.

She describes the dream as follows:

There is a valley, lying at a rather high altitude in the foothills of the Himalayan-Tibet ranges. It is surrounded by high mountains on all sides except towards the northeast, where there is a narrow opening in the mountain ranges. The valley is, therefore, bottle-shaped in contour, with the neck of the bottle to the northeast, and it widens very considerably towards the south. Up towards the northern end, close to the neck of the bottle, there is to be found a huge flat rock. There are no trees or shrubs in the valley, which is covered with a kind of coarse grass, but the sides of the mountains are covered with trees.

At the time of the full moon of Taurus, pilgrims from all the surrounding districts begin to gather; the holy men and lamas find their way into the valley and fill the southern and the middle parts, leaving the northeastern end relatively free. There, so the legend runs, gathers a group of those great Beings Who are the Custodians on Earth of God's Plan for our planet and for humanity.... This group of knowers of divinity are the main participants in the Wesak Festival. They range Themselves in the northeastern end of the valley, and in concentric circles (according to the status and grade of Their initiatory development) prepare Themselves for a great act of service. In front of the rock, looking towards the northeast, stand Those Beings Who are called by Their disciples "the Three Great Lords." These are the Christ, who stands in the center; the Lord of living forms, the Manu, Who stands on His right; and the Lord of Civilisation, Who stands on His left. These three face the rock, upon which there rests a great crystal bowl, full of water.

Those who dreamed of participating in the ceremony were aware of the exact location where they were positioned, which reflected their evolutionary status. Bailey describes the atmosphere as characterized by "demand, readiness and expectancy" as the time of the full moon approaches:

[A] stillness settles down upon the crowd, and all look towards the northeast. Certain ritualistic movements take place, in which the grouped Masters and Their disciples of all ranks take up symbolic positions, and form on the floor of the valley such significant symbols as the five-pointed star, with the Christ standing at the highest point; or a triangle, with the Christ at the apex; or a cross, and other well known formations, all of which have a deep and potent meaning. This is all done to the sound of certain chanted words and esoteric phrases, called mantrams. The expectancy in the waiting, onlooking crowds becomes very great, and the tension is real and increasing. Through the entire body of people there seems to be felt a stimulation or potent vibration which has the effect of awakening the souls of those present, fusing and blending the group into one united whole, and lifting all into a great act of spiritual demand, readiness, and expectancy. It is the climax of the world's aspiration, focused in this waiting group.

As the chanting and the rhythmic weaving grow stronger, all turn in the direction of the narrow part of the valley:

[I]n the far distance, a tiny speck can be seen in the sky. It comes nearer and nearer, and grows in clarity and definiteness of outline, until the form of the Buddha can be seen, seated in the cross-legged Buddha position, clad in His saffron-coloured robe, bathed in light and colour, and with His hand extended in blessing. When He arrives at a point exactly over the great rock, hovering there in the air over the heads of the three Great Lords, a great mantram, used only once a year, at the Festival, is intoned by the Christ, and the entire group of people in the valley fall upon their faces. This Invocation sets up a great vibration or thought current which is of such potency that it reaches up from the group of aspirants, disciples or initiates who employ it, to God Himself. It marks the supreme moment of intensive spiritual effort throughout the entire year, and the spiritual vitalization of humanity and the spiritual effects last throughout the succeeding months. The effect of this great Invocation is universal or cosmic, and serves to link us up with that cosmic centre of spiritual force from which all created beings have come. The blessing is poured forth, and the Christ—as the Representative of humanity—receives it in trust, for distribution.[97]

Then as the Buddha disappears, a bowl of water (that has been magnetized by the ceremony) is distributed to the Masters, initiates, disciples and all those present. If we believe in the possibility of the reality behind this dream, we will surely want to do all we can to participate in this event to the best of our ability. Primarily we are asked to become pure channels and released minds.

The Tibetan wrote, "No cost is too great to pay in order to be of use to the Hierarchy at the time of the full moon of May; no price is too high in order to gain the spiritual illumination which can be possible, particularly at that time."[98] He asked us to make an effort at "inner silence, introspective thought, self-control and meditation; self-forgetfulness and attentiveness to opportunity."[99]

The Wesak full moon is known as the full moon of the Buddha. The Buddha was born under the sign of Taurus, achieved enlightenment and died under the impress of this sign. He taught the means to the clarification of the mind as symbolized in the keynote of Taurus: "I see, and when the eye is opened, all is light." Throughout time religious festivals have been commemorations of events and of spiritual teachers who lived and died many years ago. As we move into the future, our understanding of religion will move away from this remembrance of things past and of spiritual teachers from antiquity, and into a recognition of the livingness of the events that are occurring now.

This observance of the Wesak Festival is part of this shift into the sense of livingness. And although this is the Festival of the Buddha, it is not the Buddha of 2,500 years ago that is being celebrated but rather the Buddha today, and the message of healing he comes to bring to our needy world. The Wesak ceremony is related to the massed intent of the Hierarchy and the massed demand of the world seekers. This massed demand is, in turn, drawn forth by the collective need of the people of the world in all lands. And everywhere today we can sense that need of humanity. Through our united effort we can make our contribution to the great work of planetary redemption that is underway.

For aeons of time humanity has stood as a break within the divine circulatory flow of energy as we turned our backs upon the light and refused to accept our responsibility that was being offered to us as the mediating kingdom between the higher spiritual worlds and the three lower kingdoms—the animal, vegetable and mineral worlds. But this break is now being repaired, or restored, as increasing numbers of people become conscious and accept responsibility for the restoration of this divine circulatory flow. Shamballa and the Hierarchy are dependent upon the evocation of the "demand" of the world seekers. Through the medium of the Buddha at the time of the Taurus full moon, this demand can be focalized and directed so that it can reach straight through to Shamballa, the bright center lying far ahead.

At this time each year we are asked to make a concerted effort to move past our inertia and do what we can to work collectively with others to bring in the light. Even though our numbers may be small, our strength is great. We must, therefore, reject the thought of our relative uselessness, insignificance and futility, and realize that now, in this critical moment, we can work potently. The world hangs in the balance.

The Buddha and the World Teacher embody the two aspects of the Second Ray of Love-Wisdom. The May full moon is consecrated to the Buddha, who embodies the wisdom aspect of the second ray, while the June full moon is dedicated to the Bodhisattva (the World Teacher, known to Christians as the Christ), the embodiment of the love aspect. At the June full moon the World Teacher links the Hierarchy with humanity. It is humanity's task to so focus its collective aspiration, in a united, invocative appeal to divinity, that great and potent energies can be precipitated on Earth.

At the time of the Gemini full moon, the World Teacher focuses human appeal, prayer and demand; transmits it in an act of spiritual intent to Shamballa[100]; and releases them in a great act of blessing. Each year at the June full moon the love of God, "the spiritual essence of solar fire," attains its highest point of expression.[101] At this time the World Teacher stands before the gathered Hierarchy and recites the Buddha's last sermon, the Beatitudes and a special Invocation.[102]

This translation of the Buddha's last sermon is taken from *The Gospel of Buddha*, compiled by Paul Carus and published in 1894.

> I am now grown old, O Ananda, and full of years;
> my journey is drawing to its close,
> I have reached the sum of my days,
> I am turning eighty years of age.
> Just as a worn-out cart cannot be made to move along without much
>   difficulty,
> so the body of the Tathagata can only be kept going with much
>   additional care.
> It is only, Ananda, when the Tathagata,
> ceasing to attend to any outward thing,
> becomes plunged into that devout meditation of heart
> which is concerned with no bodily object,
> it is only then that the body of the Tathagata is at ease.
> Therefore, O Ananda, be ye lamps unto yourselves.
> Rely on yourselves, and do not rely on external help.
> Hold fast to the truth as a lamp.
> Seek salvation alone in the truth.
> Look not for assistance to any one besides yourselves.
> And how, Ananda, can a brother be a lamp unto himself,
> rely on himself only and not on any external help,
> holding fast to the truth as his lamp
> and seeking salvation in the truth alone,
> looking not for assistance to any one besides himself?
> Herein, O Ananda, let a brother,
> as he dwells in the body, so regard the body that he,
> being strenuous, thoughtful, and mindful, may,
> whilst in the world,
> overcome the grief which arises from the body's cravings.
> While subject to sensations

let him continue so to regard the sensations that he,
being strenuous, thoughtful, and mindful, may,
whilst in the world,
overcome the grief which arises from the sensations.
And so, also, when he thinks or reasons, or feels,
let him so regard his thoughts
that being strenuous, thoughtful, and mindful he may,
whilst in the world,
overcome the grief which arises
from the craving due to ideas,
or to reasoning, or to feeling.
Those who, either now or after I am dead,
shall be lamps unto themselves,
relying upon themselves only
and not relying upon any external help,
but holding fast to the truth as their lamp,
and seeking their salvation in the truth alone,
and shall not look for assistance
to any one besides themselves,
it is they, Ananda, among my bhikkhus,
who shall reach the very height!
But they must be anxious to learn.

Since 1952 this day has also been celebrated as World Invocation Day.[103] This day is always celebrated as a day of prayer and meditation, when people make a united appeal to divinity and join together to use the Great Invocation. The use of this powerful prayer charges this day with deep spiritual significance, for it builds a channel through which light, love and power can reach and irradiate the hearts and minds of people everywhere.

The Tibetan suggests the following actions for the entire week prior to the May and the June Full Moons:

a. Link up with all disciples, aspirants, and men and women of goodwill throughout the world and in all nations, using the creative imagination.

b. Eliminate out of your consciousness all negativity, seeing yourself clearly as ranged on the side of the Forces of Light; you are, therefore, not neutral in thought. See to it also that when taking right action in the conflict against the forces of materialism you preserve ever a spirit of love for all individuals who have been swept into the vortex of their potency.

c. When meditating and invoking the Forces of Light, endeavour to forget entirely all your own personal difficulties, tragedies and problems. Disciples have to learn to carry forward their work for humanity in spite of personality stresses, strains and limitations.

d. Prepare yourselves thus for the work of the two Full Moons, keeping your objective clearly in mind and submitting yourselves to an adequate temporary discipline.

For the two days prior to the full moon, on the day of the full moon itself, and for the two succeeding days (five days) endeavour at sunrise, at noon, at five o'clock P.M., and at sunset, plus the exact time of the full moon in your own land, to say the Great Invocation with the intent to invoke, precipitate and anchor in outer manifestation the waiting Potencies. Do this aloud when possible, and in group formation whenever feasible. It is the focussed power of your unemotional thought which will bridge the present existing gap and link more closely the two worlds of spiritual activity and of human demonstration.

Repeat this activity for three days each and every month—the day prior to the full moon, the day of the full moon, and the succeeding day. As a preliminary exercise to these three days, you could take an earlier three days of preparation, and thus increase the effectiveness of your effort.[104]

CHAPTER 11

CHALLENGES ON THE PATH

A Necessary Caution

There are no hard and fast rules as to how any particular individual will be affected by his or her application to the spiritual path. We are all different, with varied life experiences that color our temperament and condition our responses. Sometimes our entry onto the path can bring us into contact with energies and forces that result in increased difficulties and imbalances that we are often ill equipped to handle. So, while it is helpful to meet life's challenges with a positive outlook, we should not create unrealistic expectations about what is in store for us as we take up this work. To do so could cause unnecessary self-judgment if we don't experience the enlightenment we seek or the instant alleviation of all difficulties.

Sometimes, in their eagerness to progress spiritually, people engage in practices that prove overly stimulating—too much meditation, intense study, breathing exercises and abstract thinking. It is unfortunate, therefore, that many teachers and books on the market today encourage such things. Too often teachers advocate intensive periods of meditation and breathing exercises for neophytes, with the intent to consciously activate the spiritual centers and force a raising of the kundalini energy. The damage caused by such practices, both physical and psychological, contributes to the mass of people who have been psychically wrecked by opening themselves up to forces and energies that they are often unable to assimilate.[105] Such situations are particularly dangerous for young people, whose lower vehicles are not fully matured and who are consequently more susceptible to the negative effects.

Some of the symptoms of this condition of overstimulation are an intense mental activity, hyperactive and erratic behavior, sexual stimulation, insomnia, a burning sensation within the spinal area, and headache.[106] It is also possible for difficult conditions to result from an opposite type of problem. Sometimes people create trouble for themselves through faulty meditation practices that render the mind passive. This passivity, which results in a numbing of the mental faculties, can leave people susceptible to the entry of powerful negative energies that can play havoc with their lives. This lulling within the brain cells can sometimes work out in delusions, psychic visions and, in extreme cases, the cultivation of the "messiah complex," in which the individual believes him- or herself to be a spokesperson for the Masters and even higher, extraterrestrial spiritual Beings.

Spiritual training should be undertaken cautiously, while living as natural, poised and balanced a life as possible. If overstimulation occurs, a solution must be found. The best policy is to give up all spiritual work, including reading and prayer, for as long as the conditions persist and until such time as the bodies have been able to "seal" up the portals of entrance for the stimulating and/or negative energies. During such times it can be helpful to concentrate upon practical, physical plane matters—working, gardening, exercising, doing community service, and living a normal and active life. Allowing the consciousness to continually drift off into mystical reveries is not helpful; one's time would be better spent concentrating upon a practical study that is of interest. Then, as healing occurs, the person can gradually resume the spiritual work, always remaining attentive and watchful for the possible recurrence of problems. The familiar fable of the tortoise and the hare is helpful to remember as we strive to "make haste slowly."[107]

Perseverance

Problems can often arise after the initial infatuation with the path fades and life settles into an established rhythm. Then sometimes the very ordinariness of life itself can prove difficult and the need to keep on becomes one of our greatest challenges. To simply endure and keep going forward when life has lost its luster calls for a condition within consciousness that is not related to age but rather to spiritual maturity. We long for forward progress into greater light and livingness, but often all we find is an essential sameness. We compare ourselves to others and to the great teachers, then despair at times in the comparison. We palpably sense the tremendous road still to be traveled upon the path and we falter on the way. Despite years of study and application to our spiritual disciplines, the progress made can appear minuscule and totally insufficient in comparison to the need that we sense all around us.

We find ourselves fed up with the process, impatient and demanding, like a petulant child. It is here that we may succumb to the lower aspects of our personality nature and pass onto a byway, a personality detour, and become enmeshed within the machinations of our particular line of least resistance. We lose much time and opportunity in this process and make mistakes, but we can also learn valuable lessons that will hold us in good stead in the future.

Sometimes the best we can do when confronted with life's challenges is simply to persevere. Far too often in life we run from situations only to find ourselves having to confront the same lessons at a later time. Perseverance is often the course of wisdom that enables a rhythm to be built into the fabric of our lives. This rhythm carries us forward even when we don't feel like going. It does, however, take time and discipline to develop these rhythms.

Modern life moves quickly and people become distracted and have little patience for qualities that require a measure of patience and solitude to unfold. Too often, we are intent upon the attainment of outer, tangible goals, seeing little merit in the eternal verities and achievements that appear nebulous and unproven. People are easily bored and seek constant change in all aspects of their lives, including the spiritual. Many people move from path to path and group to group with alarming rapidity, in search of quick and easy results, never taking the time to penetrate beneath the surface of any of them.

Spiritual goals, however, take time and dedication to achieve. You can't, for example, buy initiation or attain spiritual realization through a quick course that will lead to any real and lasting developments within your consciousness. Instead it often takes long years of steady, quiet practice, often with few outer results. But it is also true that many people today, especially the young, are coming into incarnation already prepared and fully able to take up the path, having attained a real measure of spiritual development in previous lifetimes.

It is often found that as we take up the spiritual path with determination, many factors will conspire, both within ourselves and within our environment, to stop us and to throw us off track. The forces of the personality are very strong and will not easily give way to the rhythms of the soul. If you doubt this, all you have to do is make a serious effort to apply yourself to this path and you will find out for yourself. You will be tested repeatedly, in ways that you may never have expected.

At the outset it is helpful to understand that we are never given more than we can handle, even though in the midst of the crisis this may not appear to be the case. At such times we often become reactive and sink into the personality self and its negative aspects. If we are not careful this condition may bar us from learning the lesson and taking the opportunity that is being offered to us. One of the most important things that we learn by passing through these crisis situations is how to meet them with greater maturity and wisdom, with equanimity and strength. Because crises shake up the very foundations of our lives, they bring to birth new qualities and opportunities that lead us forward in ways that we might never have experienced otherwise.

The New Psychology and Spiritual Healing

As a result of the present stimulation mental and emotional imbalances have increased exponentially. Some of these conditions could in effect be viewed as a consequence of a premature "penetration" or opening of doors in perception.

The whole field of psychology is passing through a transition period as it shifts to meet the changing and increasing needs of people today. Mental health is a subtle science and we know relatively little about the complexities and depth of the mind. As more psychologists begin to investigate and incorporate the study and research of the energy bodies and the teaching on the seven rays into their practice, the whole field will expand and deepen.

In the future, psychology will be the preeminent science, for it will come to be recognized as the means whereby we can unfold our full potential. Psychologists will come to understand that the goal of all successful analysis is integration and alignment of the lower threefold personality vehicles with the overshadowing energy of the soul. The whole art of spiritual and natural healing is in its infancy, but it will come into prominence in the coming age and esoteric psychology will be an integral part of this work.[108] The end result of all spiritual practice is the increasing ability to heal. In this regard the Tibetan wrote, "Those who use this power *only* for the sake of the little ones, taking and seeking no personal reward, can manifest the ancient way to heal...."[109] As humanity unfolds its spiritual potential, many more individuals will come to possess the power to alleviate suffering. And increasingly healing groups will emerge, composed of individuals who will work quietly, behind the scenes, with little or no outer recognition—using the techniques of esoteric healing.[110]

A growing number of physicians and psychologists are beginning to incorporate more natural methods of healing and preventative measures in their work. These techniques do not often yield the quick fix that our contemporary world so often demands—and that the medical establishment is eager to offer—for the alleviation of pain and suffering. But over time, in some cases, more natural methods of healing can lead to an enhanced sense of well-being. And while psychiatric medications have done much to help people whose lives would be completely unmanageable otherwise, there are alternatives and medication should not be looked upon as a panacea. More research is needed with treatments moving outside the bounds of the powerful pharmaceutical industry. Many people today are embracing natural, less invasive treatments that produce fewer negative side effects than traditional psychiatric medications. The incredible openness and experimentation that is occurring at this time within the field of alternative healing is exciting and holds much promise for new techniques for the alleviation of suffering.

It must be noted that spiritual practices should not be combined with the use of psychiatric medication. People would be well advised to hold off initiating any activities along this line until such time as they can give up the medication without any harm to themselves. Meditation brings powerful energies into the brain cells and the stimulation can easily have adverse consequences upon people whose natures lack the necessary balance. And of course the same warning holds true for any other type of mind-altering substance.

CHAPTER 12

DISCRIMINATION AND LIBERATION

The Buddha encouraged each one of us to "be a lamp unto our own feet." In other words, he asked us, as far as possible, to think for ourselves and to follow truth, not personalities. Discrimination is an essential quality to be cultivated in this process as it enables us to look beneath the surface of outer events, to become self-reliant and therefore learn to see life more clearly.

Sometimes, however, in the effort to avoid the dangers of criticism, seekers fail to develop and exercise their discriminative powers, erroneously believing that to be truly spiritual demands a general openness and fluidity in regard to people and events. After all, the great teachers asked us to turn the other cheek and to be "meek." But perhaps we suffer under the weight of faulty translations and the misinterpretation of ancient injunctions that lead in turn to an unduly passive and "negative" approach to life and its events. We forget that the greatest expression of love that ever walked on Earth demonstrated many instances of will and strong action in his life of service. He did, however, maintain an inclusive love for all humanity that remained the underlying quality behind all that he did.

Seekers who fail to develop their discriminative powers may find themselves entering into situations that would be best avoided. Caution is necessary in spiritual work. Christ told us that before his second coming the world would be awash with false prophets, and so it is today. It is a good idea, therefore, to be cautious and investigate any teaching or teacher with a discriminating eye before becoming involved; otherwise we might find ourselves walking down a slippery road. In this day it is easy to be taken in by the slick and seemingly noble rhetoric put forward by many individuals and groups. It is best, therefore, to read widely and observe closely. Many spurious teachers and groups make claims that can dupe naïve and indiscriminate seekers, distorting the spiritual truths that are struggling to come to the light of day. These claims demonstrate the very real dangers of the astral plane with its propensity to delude.

Many seemingly sincere people have impressions that appear quite real, which they claim emanate from high spiritual sources. Unfortunately, often these contacts are with "astral shells"—forms or images of the great teachers that exist quite vividly upon the astral plane of awareness but have no basis in reality. We have to beware of the power, the psychically induced pseudo-spiritual power and magnetism, that teachers who are in touch with these astral shells wield—either consciously or unconsciously. If we are not careful, we might find ourselves unwittingly pulled into a web from which it is difficult to escape. At the very least we might find ourselves sidetracked, and at this time when all hands are needed, this is something we can not afford.

Even though some people may yearn for recognition by a teacher, and even think they merit it, the truth is that if they were ever able to contact a real teacher, the vibration would "crush them," as a fellow traveler on the path likes to say. The august intensity that emanates from a Master of the Wisdom would prove shattering and dangerous because of the coarseness of the unready seeker's lower vehicles which are unable to withstand the vibration. Also it must be recognized that the great teachers are not eager to make our acquaintance, because in the beginning of that relationship we pose more of a liability than a gain to the work that needs to be done. We are therefore advised to cease from any focus upon contact with the teachers. But when the student is ready, a teacher will appear who can provide the needed stimulation to take the next step.

At a certain stage upon the path we are often guided by someone on the physical plane who serves as a mentor or role model to us. This person is clearly not a Master of the Wisdom, but rather someone who is assigned the task of dealing with probationary students. There are many people in the world today working in this way. We are fortunate if we find such a person, because we learn so much from him or her. Such people provide us with the tangible evidence of just what it means to live at a point of spiritual tension, in alignment with hierarchical intent. They make the theoretical real. These relationships, while highly rewarding on one level, can prove exceedingly difficult on another, because we are brought into association with a powerful energy field to which we are unaccustomed and to which our vehicles must adjust. Initially this causes disruption and a painful process of change and reorientation, as we adjust to the heightened vibratory rate.

The Rites of Contact

The relationship between students and the inner teachers is based upon the work that needs to be done and is not related to personalities and the problems that manifest upon the physical plane. We must resolve these things ourselves. We must learn to stand within that space where everything is revealed. The teachers are not concerned with our personalities, or with our faults, limitations or preferences. They look only for our light and willingness to subordinate our personalities to the Plan. As one teacher said of the student/teacher relationship, "Know us for sane and balanced men, who teach as we taught on earth, not flattering our pupils but disciplining them. We lead them on, not forcing them forward by feeding their ambitions by promises of power, but giving them information and leading them to use it in their work, knowing that right use of knowledge leads to experience and achievement of the goal."[111] The teachers look at us from the perspective of long cycles of time, over the course of a series of different lives. We only matter, ultimately, to the extent that we can provide a means of helping to forward the spiritual work in the world (in all its myriad manifestations) and lifting a little of the burden from those who can then be freed to take on other responsibilities.

Often people think that if they are just good enough, obedient enough, and selfless enough that one day a Master will contact them as a token of appreciation or an accolade of recognition for the good work that they have done, but that is not how it works. It is safe to assume that if a Master expends the necessary force to contact one of his probationary students, it generally comes in the form of a warning and the need for correction. Sometimes, however, in the case of a valued and trusted worker who has made considerable progress, a word or impression from the Master may make a difference, may turn the tide so that that individual can be encouraged to undertake a piece of work that may prove useful to the ashram, as was the case with Alice Bailey. But generally we are expected to figure things out for ourselves and solve our own problems—for it is in the solving of our problems that we grow and learn many valuable lessons. Alice Bailey also asked us to remember that though we receive no response from a Master to a sincere plea for help, we should not necessarily assume that our request was not heard. We may not receive the response at the moment that we request it or in the form that we might expect, but it is safe to assume that we have been heard.

This seeming lack of contact or interest upon the part of the great teachers in regard to their students' personal lives is a hard teaching for some people to understand and accept. The essential paradox, however, is that we only merit the time and attention of an inner teacher when we have reached a level of consciousness that no longer thinks in those terms. The contact becomes possible as the consciousness becomes so decentralized and detached from personal concerns and special messages that the individual identity begins to fade into the background under the unfolding panorama of life itself.

The Problems of Devotion

The problem of the disciple is to reach a point where he is not hindered or held back by any human being and yet so to handle himself as far as attitude is concerned that he hurts no one in the process of withdrawal. The outer personality claims of attachment are oft so powerful that their clatter and their rattle prevent awareness of the golden thread which links us with another soul. Likewise, overestimation of another person can act as a real hindrance. The chains must break, leaving only a golden thread between each soul—a golden thread which cannot break.

Alice Bailey, *Discipleship in the New Age, Vol. I*

No devotee is independent; he is a prisoner of an idea or a person.[112]

Alice Bailey, *Discipleship in the New Age, Vol. II*

Devotion to a teacher, or to a cause, can become selfish if it blocks our contact with people or other groups, leading us to focus instead upon our special work, our special mission to the world and our special relationship with the teacher. Finding the right way in which to channel our devotion is one of the challenges of the path. The shift that is occurring as we move out of the Piscean influence into that of Aquarius could, in a certain sense, be characterized by the shift from the quality of *devotion* to that of *brotherhood*. Brotherhood is the essence of the Plan that is working out at this time on our planet. Devotion, if we allow it to unduly condition us, weakens our resolve and creates dependency, holding us in the grip of the outgoing Piscean energies. This is never good, and no true teacher would demand this or encourage devotion in his or her students. The quality of brotherhood, on the other hand, holds out the possibility of greatly expanding our worldview and integrating us within the one humanity. A sense of brotherhood doesn't do away with the need for leaders, but it does place the onus of responsibility upon our leaders to move in concert with the new energies of a group paradigm that supports, rather than seeks to dominate, the individuals in the group.

In regard to the problems associated with devotion, it is interesting to read what the Tibetan, in one of his very few personal references, wrote of an apparent life of failure that he experienced a few lifetimes ago. He said,

> Several lives ago, my Master saw in me a weakness. It was one of which I was quite unaware and it was in fact a quality which I regarded as a strength and which I hugged to myself as a virtue. I was then a young man, anxious to help my Master and humanity but, in the last analysis, I was very keen about myself as an aspirant and very pleased with myself—cloaking this satisfaction under the garb of a reiterated humility. The Master poured into me His strength and energy and so stimulated me that what I thought was a virtue and what I had denied and repudiated as a vice, proved my undoing. I symbolically crashed to earth through the very weight of my weakness. You might well ask what this weakness was? It was my love for my Master which was my undoing. He pointed out to me after the failure that my love for Him was in reality based upon pride in myself and a profound satisfaction with myself as an aspirant and a disciple. This I violently denied and was grieved that He should so misunderstand me. I proved Him to be right, eventually, through a life of failure and the depth of my egotism. I learnt through that failure but I lost much time from the standpoint of useful service. I found that I was really serving myself and not humanity. From similar mistakes, I seek to save you, for time is a great factor in service. For the masses of humanity, time is not of very great importance; but for the servers of the race, it matters much. Lose not time, therefore, in undue self-analysis, self-depreciation or self-defence. Go forward with discrimination where your unfoldment is concerned, aid with love and understanding where your group is concerned. Where I, your teacher, am concerned, give to my words the attention which is due and endeavor to cooperate with me. I shall then some day have the joy of welcoming you to the 'Secret Place' where all true servers and initiates must eventually meet and unite.[113]

Impressions from the Inner Planes

The discussion of inner experiences is something about which most sincere seekers are naturally reticent. There are so many false claims being made that the sensitive seeker usually keeps his own counsel in this regard. But sometimes, as part of the process of developing group consciousness and a cooperative spirit, a sharing of these experiences can prove helpful and expands the bonds between group members. The Tibetan teacher brought forth a wealth of information that helps us to distinguish truth from falsity. However, the general public finds itself often in the unfortunate situation of being informed about such things, via books and lectures, by those individuals whose contacts are not real and whose focus is upon personalities, not service to humanity.

At times impressions can come through from the inner planes upon waking. This time provides an open door of perception through which a merging of the inner and outer worlds becomes possible. The normal limitations recede and the mind is caught up in a deeper reality that grasps large vistas, synthetic wholes, in a seeming totality of perception that is rarely possible in the normal waking state. The challenge then is to pull through and capture or concretize this information in a form that is understandable to the waking consciousness, without losing the thread, or connection, in the process of manifestation. Sometimes people experience powerful inpourings of kundalini energy during the night. These experiences can be frightening at first because of the intensity of the stimulation.

Alice Bailey relayed an interesting and amusing story in her *Unfinished Autobiography* about an attempt to contact the Tibetan teacher. She wrote of a very sincere individual who was an associate of hers who wanted to go to Tibet to contact the Tibetan. He wanted to make this journey to inform the Tibetan that he should go easier on Alice because she was severely overworked. Bailey laughed and told him that if he truly wanted to contact the Tibetan that he could do so from where he was if he took the proper steps within consciousness to bring it about. She said that he didn't have to run off to Tibet to make that contact. This man, however, was persistent in his intention and during his second trip a lama came down into India to meet him, surrounded by other high lamas from the area. The people of the community all bowed in respect to the visitor. The lama inquired about the work that was going on in New York and asked after Alice Bailey and gave the man two large bundles of incense for her. This lama told Alice's friend that he was the abbot of a large monastery in Tibet. Later, Alice's friend recounted this story to a Tibetan General from Darjeeling who said he must have been mistaken, as this abbot was a very great and holy man who would never venture into India, especially to meet with an Occidental. However, it was later confirmed that indeed the meeting had taken place. But at the time, this man never realized that the great lama was, in fact, Master Djwhal Khul who worked with Alice Bailey. Bailey said that this example shows us that we could quite easily be within the presence of a Master but not realize it, unless we had developed the inner mechanism of recognition. This story might even encourage certain types of people to run off to India and Tibet in the hope of contacting a teacher. They would most likely be disappointed.

The Tibetan tells us that a sensitive response to impression is dependent upon similarity of vibration and karma.[114] As we move to contact our inner group, we are likewise coming under the influence of the inner teachers who stand at the center of those groups. Alignment with that center can manifest in a feeling of inner expansion, a fullness within the lower vehicles—if only for a fleeting moment before we quickly lose the connection and find ourselves dropping back into the mundane and known. But over time the vibratory contact becomes more frequent, of varied types, and of longer duration which requires adjustments in the vehicles in order to be sustained. The individual sets up the right condi-tions, or in the parlance of the teachings "engenders an aura upon which the highest impressions can play." The teacher, from his side, works on the student's subtle vehicles and applies stimulation as needed, particularly during periods of meditation and during the hours of sleep.

Over time, the Tibetan tells us that we will come to distinguish between the different types of vibrations to which we are subject—for example, those that emanate from the soul, from the ashram, from the Master, and from our discipleship group.[115] Each vibration has a different "coloring," a different vibratory feel and note that is registered in the different centers depending upon the nature of the energy. These vibrations, which the Tibetans call "the gift waves" of the spirit, can come upon us during our periods of meditation, but also at any time during the day. The progressive developments within consciousness that take place between the inner teachers and their students are explained in considerable detail at the end of the book *Discipleship in the New Age, Vol. I*, in a section entitled "The Six Stages of Discipleship."

CHAPTER 13

INITIATION

The work of initiation is to enable a man [or woman] to live ever at the centre, but to act as a distributor of divine energy in any direction and—after the later initiations—in all directions.

Alice Bailey, *A Treatise on White Magic*

INTRODUCTORY THOUGHTS

When we consider the process of initiation, we enter into a subject that is shrouded in mystery and considerable confusion. Due to the potency of the energies released during the initiation rites, down through the ages these teachings have remained secret—hidden and protected from the unready within ancient texts, symbolic writings and rituals. Today some of the veils surrounding this teaching are being lifted on account of the sheer number of people who are ready for the training.

Initiation relates to the ability to stand in the light, and from within that light to penetrate into increasingly deeper manifestations of it. Initiation has been defined simply as "to enter into"[116] a new state of consciousness. There are five primary initiations for humanity, yet there are no hard and fast lines of demarcation between them. The path is one of constant mutations and recapitulations as past, present and future blend and weave together in a never-ending mosaic of transformation. Sometimes we are moving forward into the light, while at other moments all appears futile and dark as we move through what has come to be known as the hill-and-valley experience of the path.

By the end of the age two-thirds of humanity will have taken one or another of the initiations.[117] According to the wisdom teachings, one of the primary reasons why the World Teacher is coming forward at this time is to help clarify initiation so that it will no longer be a mystery.

THE FIVE INITIATIONS

The initiatory process begins with the tremendous inner re-orientation in consciousness that occurs at the time of the first initiation when we first place our feet upon the path of return and the inner worlds become real and powerful to us. This initiation is known as the Birth.[118] It is interesting in this regard to observe the emphasis that evangelical Christians place upon the concept of being "born again" to the new life in Christ. This new birth is symbolic of the start of a long inner journey of transformation.

The soul communicates with "its reflection" (the personality) through rhythmic response, and therefore as we begin to institute a measure of order and discipline in our daily affairs, we facilitate the inflow of energy from the soul. We can see this happening today with the increasing focus upon the physical disciplines by so many people through sports, body training, vegetarianism, the various yogas, and other forms of meditation and spiritual practices. These measures all contribute towards refinement at the physical level that prepares the body for spiritual work. The reorientation of the life that occurs as a result of the taking of the first initiation is often preceded by a period of pain, disruption, and a weariness with the world. It is a time for decision, an exquisite time when the consciousness hovers on the borderline of revelation, and with a little effort the tenor of the life can shift to a higher level.

As mentioned earlier, the path is long and the human being unfolds through a long series of lives. The rate of progress varies from individual to individual; therefore some people move forward more quickly than others. This will not necessarily mean that they are smarter, but they may be wiser—they may make fewer mistakes and find themselves consequently less burdened with the trappings that an older soul (from the angle of time spent in the evolutionary process) is experiencing. And while many old souls may have highly developed gifts at the level of the personality, they nonetheless still struggle to learn the lessons of detachment and humility that the Christ achieved aeons ago. They find themselves delayed within one cul-de-sac or another, but at any time they may make those decisions that will serve to reorient them quickly within the current of life. Then rapid progress can be made and great strides taken within a single lifetime, allowing the individual to move forward with speed, as in the conversion experiences of certain souls, most notably St. Paul.

But it can equally be true that many lives can pass in which apparently little or no progress is being made. These are sometimes called lives of interlude, and they are generally times when the changes that are occurring are more internal, taking place within the recesses of consciousness. It is helpful, therefore, to reserve judgment in respect to the people who pass through our lives in the recognition that some are on the ebb and others on the flow within their particular cycle of manifestation.[119] All cycles are important and contribute to the expansion of the life. These points are merely touched upon to give some inkling of the complexity of this entire question of evolutionary development and the determination of one's place upon the path.

Vast numbers of people will take the first initiation during this planetary cycle of the Aquarian Age. But increasing numbers are also preparing for the second initiation, so that humanity is now facing the second initiation on a "relatively large scale." Thousands of people will pass through this experience during the present cycle.[120] This initiation, sometimes known as the Baptism, is related to the control and harnessing of the fluid and water-like astral or emotional vehicle. The battle upon the astral plane is intense at this stage of development and creates many conflicting emotions that can result in much confusion in life. These conflicts and struggles make the second initiation a long and difficult undertaking. Therefore, one of the primary qualities needed for the taking of the second initiation is perseverance.

Many lives must pass between the taking of the first and second initiations, lives of apparent darkness and slow, quiet, inner growth. At the second initiation the individual demonstrates emotional control—not under all circumstances and situations, but rather as a general tendency. He or she learns to make use of the mind as a "dispelling agent," a means whereby the fogs and mists of the astral plane can be dissipated. The Tibetan wrote of this stage:

> Perhaps you prefer the slower and easier way. If that is so, it is entirely your own affair, and you are still on your way. You are still a constructive and useful person. I am simply here facing you with one of the crises which come in the life of all disciples, wherein choices have to be made that are determining for a cycle, but for a cycle only. It is pre-eminently a question of speed and of organizing for speed. This means eliminating the non-essentials and concentrating on the essentials—the inner essentials, as they concern the soul and its relation to the personality, and the outer ones as they concern you and your environment.[121]

The most difficult period upon the path is between the second and third initiations; this is the time when the real battle for the control of the personality by the soul takes place. The stage following the second initiation is beautifully symbolized by the Sagittarian experience, in which the individual moves rapidly across the plains, from point to point and goal to goal. The individual becomes aware of the essential simplicity of life as it exists within the higher realms of consciousness. Oneness, synthesis, the interconnectedness of all life—these are the developments that begin to take place at this stage.

Up until the taking of the third initiation, mistakes can be made that arrest the progress and stand as blinders to the light. Forward progress upon the path is not yet assured. We are still potentially dangerous and viewed as unstable from the perspective of the inner teachers. At this stage we would be well advised to cultivate the relinquishment of gain as counseled in the *Bhagavad Gita* by learning to act without attachment to the fruits of our actions.

Prior to the third initiation, this pride of personality can pose a very real barrier to the soul's advancement. That is one of the reasons why detachment is needed. It is a symbolic truth that we must all face the One Initiator empty-handed—free from the "riches" of personality accumulations. The attainments and skills that unfold as the person develops spiritually can easily cause attachment and an inflated sense of self. Spiritual energy is pouring in, latent talents begin to blossom, and quite often the individual is charged with a sense of purpose and a desire to manifest that purpose in the world.

Within the ranks of the spiritual Hierarchy, the third initiation is known as the first real initiation—the earlier two initiations being referred to simply as "initiations of the threshold." A terrific voltage passes through the initiate's body at the taking of the third initiation. After this initiation the main thrust of the individual's life, his "ashramic service," is "to learn the uses of the ajna centre and consciously and with right understanding to work with, absorb, transmute and distribute energy."[122] He is a scientist, working on the mental plane.

As the individual moves forward towards the fourth initiation, all of the gifts and talents at the level of the personality that have been developed over the long course of many lifetimes (the "rich young man"[123] in Biblical terminology) are renounced. Even the house of the soul itself, sometimes called the causal body, is destroyed. This destruction of the causal body (which is said to be a "house" of great beauty) is the ultimate renunciation that occurs at this initiation and is said to be the "culminating renunciation and the climaxing gesture of ages of small renunciations."[124] This renunciation signals that the individual no longer has anything within him- or herself that relates to the lower three worlds.

We can really know little of such things and states of consciousness until we arrive at this stage, but it is helpful, nonetheless, to consider them, as this serves to stretch the fabric and contours of our minds and enriches our fragmentary understanding of that which is to come. The fourth initiation is the time of the shattering of everything for which the personality has stood and that it has held dear, and from a certain perspective it is said to appear as a great loss. But that sense of loss is only the temporary effect of an interior process of spiritual realignment leading to a great liberation within consciousness.

The fifth initiation is called the Revelation. Revelation is the process that leads us from darkness into light and, consequently, into a vaster vision. In the teachings of the Ageless Wisdom this initiation has been awesomely described as "the rising out of the ocean of matter into the clear light of day."[125]

* * * * *

We do not need to attend school or university to undertake training for initiation. As mentioned, spiritual development is achieved primarily through individual effort. There are, however, a number of esoteric schools functioning in the world at this time that are providing their students with valuable training. The Arcane School, one of the most established and well regarded of all the schools, is a correspondence course that was started by Alice Bailey and has proved invaluable for many students throughout the world. It offers a systematic and progressive training in meditation with guidelines for study and service—these being the three pillars of the School's curriculum.

The many individuals in the world who have passed through the present esoteric schools and movements are building the foundation for the eventual appearance of the new and coming schools of initiation. The esoteric schools that will emerge sometime after the externalization of the Hierarchy takes place[126] will demonstrate a new and different educational model to the world.

Schools of initiation were always part of the mystery traditions down the ages, and the time is now approaching when they will again come into manifestation, upon a higher turn of the spiral, to meet the needs of the coming generations who will be ready to undergo the rigorous training methods that these schools will impart. There will be two tiers to the coming schools, the preparatory and the advanced. In the eyes of the outer world, the preparatory schools will appear quite similar in form to contemporary universities. They will adhere to many of the standard academic courses, but they will also impart the foundations of esotericism to their students via a study of the constitution of the human being and numerous other topics such as astronomy, astrology, the laws of electricity, past lives, the rays and mediumship. In the advanced schools the training will deepen substantially. Their most important vehicle of spiritual growth will be through the practice of meditation.

CHAPTER 14

GROUP INITIATION

> Let it be constantly remembered that the new discipleship is primarily an experiment in group work and that its main objective is not the perfecting of the individual disciple in the group….The individuals are intended to supplement each other and complement each other and in the aggregate of their qualities should eventually provide a group capable of useful, spiritual expression and one through which spiritual energy can flow for the helping of humanity.
>
> Alice Bailey, *Discipleship in the New Age, Vol. I*

In earlier and simpler times, when there were not so many people who demonstrated fitness for initiation, the teachers were able to work individually with their students (primarily subjectively, but also at times upon the physical plane), giving them personal attention and suggestions. As the number of candidates for initiation swelled over the course of the last centuries, coupled with the intensity of the preparatory work that has been going on within the Hierarchy itself and the overwhelming reality of world need, the demands upon the teachers' time became so great that they could no longer work individually with students and the process of group initiation was instituted.

This shift marked a dramatic departure from the past. We are living through the formative stages in this work, maneuvering through uncharted territory. Surely over time the whole process will become clearer, for Aquarius is a sign of group consciousness, group work and group initiation. Collectively the group acts as a chalice through which the energy flows.

Group initiation means that each time we move forward upon the path or penetrate more deeply into the mysteries of life, we do so in the company of our group. We must be careful, therefore, not to interpret group initiation too concretely for this will cloud our understanding. Group initiation is primarily a subjective experience. Although the group itself exists within our consciousness, group members often come together to work upon the physical plane. Initiation is taken by groups of individuals working along the same soul ray line who are taught, as a group, by a Master along that ray. Our spiritual group is generally a combination of people we know, apparent strangers, and people we may have met at one time or another. Sometimes a lack of outer physical plane affiliation can allow for a freer exchange of soul energy, without the complications that so often characterize physical plane relationships.

Each member of the group handles his own affairs, undertakes his own discipline and training—for it ever holds true that we are primarily self-taught and solve our own problems. The attitude of the group members is renouncing in nature, "seeking nothing, asking nothing, hoping nothing for the separated self." As the individual, personal will of the group members is transmuted into a collective group will, the members find that all of their needs are taken care of.

The most radiant and magnetic groups, those that can offer the most powerful service to the Plan, are composed of highly self-aware people who are able to subordinate their individual predilections to the greater good of the group. Madame Blavatsky likened such groups to "the fingers on one hand." She also said the disciples must be tuned by the guru as the strings of a lute, each different from the others, yet each emitting sounds in harmony with all.[127] Mary Bailey[128] coined the phrase "the group disciple" to describe the state of consciousness that conditions those groups that are paving new paths in planetary consciousness.

The natural care and reticence with which we approach the subject of initiation has to be balanced by the recognition of our responsibility to help others, on account of the sheer magnitude of the need that exists at this time. As mentioned, since the teachers' attention is turned in other directions, the outer physical plane groups have had to assume some of the responsibilities that at an earlier time were not theirs. The bulk of the preliminary training of aspirants to the path now falls to groups of individuals who have progressed somewhat further along the way and have therefore incurred greater responsibilities. This guidance, coupled with the teaching available in book form, in the esoteric schools, and that which transpires upon the inner planes, is sufficient to meet the need at this time.

The Hierarchy is composed of individuals at varying stages of spiritual development, and so are the groups that are being prepared for initiation. This is what makes the work so powerful and far-reaching in nature. If all of the workers were functioning upon the same level of consciousness, the rich and many-textured layers of creativity that hierarchical work always exhibits would not be possible. This diversity among the group members enables it to have a wide range of contact. The more aligned members of the group intuit the Plan, the experienced workers then coordinate that Plan within the group, and the newer members carry out the work upon the physical plane.[129]

The inner teachers depend upon humanity to help them in the work that needs to be done. They do not know, as fully as we, the specific needs of men and women today, because that is not where their focus of attention lies. It is the individuals who are actively working in the world who have a deeper and clearer understanding of just what needs to be done and how to do it. It is helpful for us to remember this, for it can serve to cut away the sense of inadequacy that so often colors spiritual seekers.

We are all needed, we can all contribute, and at this time of spiritual emergency, all sense of our inability to measure up has to be eliminated. Hierarchical work is, in the truest sense of the term, group work in which each individual has his or her place and assigned task to contribute towards the smooth functioning of the greater whole. This work, which is the One work in which we are all engaged, constitutes what is known as the great chain of Hierarchy.

Master Djwhal Khul's Group

One interesting aspect of the work that Master Djwhal Khul undertook with Alice Bailey's cooperation involved contacting and teaching a small group of people over a period of twenty years. This work was interesting because it demonstrated the real joys, as well as the difficulties, that arise through the course of spiritual group training. Although the Tibetan chose the members of this group himself, he never contacted any of the individuals upon the physical plane. He sought them out instead through the light that they each manifested in the world. In some cases, the Tibetan had long-established karmic relationships with the individuals chosen, and in other cases he thought that the individuals could prove helpful in the work that he wanted to see done within the world. The Tibetan was able to work at a distance (from Tibet) to penetrate into the minds of the group members and, in a very real sense, to know them more fully than they knew themselves. Each person in the group was assigned special individual meditations as well as group meditation work and other spiritual techniques that the Tibetan gave out. The purpose of this work was to unite the group subjectively so that they could work together in a more powerful way to serve humanity.

The Tibetan corresponded with the group, via Alice Bailey, over a period of some twenty years. The group was not a success in terms of what the Tibetan had originally intended, and it was eventually disbanded. But out of the accumulated materials received by the group came the publication of the two volumes of teaching contained within the *Discipleship in the New Age* books as well as the works *Telepathy and the Etheric Vehicle* and *Glamour: A World Problem*. The *Discipleship in the New Age* books provide

insight into the inner lives of a group of individuals who were attempting to follow a spiritual path under the direct guidance of a
Master of the Wisdom. The failure of this group stemmed primarily from the under-activity of the heart centers of the group members. As a result of this failing, the group was unable to integrate
fully and their consequent service to the world was limited.

The following is an excerpt from a letter received by a member
of the Tibetan's group. This example gives the reader a sampling
of the type of insights that a Master of the Wisdom can bring to
bear upon an individual student under his care.

BROTHER SERVER:

I have watched you for some years now, little as you may have
suspected it. It was under my definitely applied impression that you
found your way into my group of disciples in which you now work,
and at the same time you found your destined field of service. I am
glad to welcome you into this group of students. The personal touch
is wise with you for you neither fear nor crave it.

In the life of every aspirant, there comes a life wherein he finds
the group to which he belongs. I refer to the inner group of disciples
and the outer group of servers with whom he can and must cooperate.
When these two discoveries synchronise (which is not always the
case) much time is saved and the opportunity is great. This has been
the case with you, and this I believe you are beginning to realise.

Your soul ray, my brother, is the first, and your personality ray
is the third. Owing to the pressure of the times and of the work for
this immediate cycle, you may have heard it said that I am relieving
some of the Teachers on the inner side and thus setting Them free
for wider and more exacting service. I am handling some of Their
pupils for Them and preparing some of Their aspirants (whom They
have been watching) for the stage of accepted discipleship. In this
last category you now find yourself. It was the coming under my
influence subjectively that led you to the realisation that the deepening of your love nature was, for you, the next step in your equipping
yourself for service. Your ray combinations necessitated this and my
second ray influence, therefore, helped. There is not an aspirant in
the world who could not well intensify his divine love nature, not his

astral emotional love nature. But you need to comprehend always the reason for any development and hence my explanation.

You have come a long distance quite rapidly upon the Path lately, and have definitely increased both your vibratory capacity and your influence. Some years of potent service are possible to you and again another explanation is in order. He Whom you will some day know as your Master when admitted in full consciousness into His group of disciples (the Master M.) is the head of all esoteric schools in the world at this time. Hence you can see why you found your way into my group of disciples and why also you are working actively and fruitfully in its executive and organisational end. It is in line with your inner group force and this, rightly understood and used, can make of you a useful focal point for the Master's energy in the place where you have chosen to serve. You must learn to differentiate, therefore, as time goes on and your sensitivity increases, between:

1. The vibratory influence (incoming and outgoing) of your own soul.
2. The vibratory influence (incoming and outgoing) of this particular group of disciples.
3. The vibratory influence (incoming and outgoing) of the esoteric schools.
4. The vibratory influence (incoming and outgoing) of the head of all esoteric groups, the Master Morya.

This you will not be able to do for some time yet, but the developing of this type of sensitivity is, for you, a needed unfoldment, and will come eventually, if you will follow my instructions with care, and let true love increasingly sweep through the lower personal self. It can sweep through, my brother, because (as you rightly feel) you do know somewhat of the nature of love. It is, however, one thing to love, and another thing to be a channel of the love of the soul and of the group."[130]

Surely each one of us can find aspects of ourselves within this group, while studying these letters, for the individuals concerned were all struggling with similar issues that confront us today. They were not all high initiates. The focus of the changes that each individual was asked to make by the Tibetan were never commands, and neither were they enforced through any means. Each person, therefore, was left free to adhere to the group requirements or not, depending upon his or her personal inclination. If they did not do the work, which primarily consisted of a meditative practice and the occasional writing of papers, they generally dropped out of the group of their own accord. The Tibetan's goal in this work was to help create an integrated group that the Masters could use for specialized work during this transition period. This is still the goal today.

Although the groups are many, their underlying objective is one. Within the realm of consciousness there is a blending and merging of the many strands within the one strand, a harmonizing of the many notes within the one sound and a blending of the many colors into the medley of the rainbow bridge.

The groups that are presently scattered throughout all parts of the world have been compared to germinating seeds, taking root "below" and bearing fruit "upwards." As this work proceeds it will eventually produce a flowering that will "cover the earth with verdure." As the Tibetan wrote, "One small plant which, in its turn, succeeds in producing a seed, through rightful fruition can thus reproduce itself in multiple order. Be not therefore unduly impressed by the smallness of the effort. A tiny seed is a potent force—if duly tended, rightly nurtured and ripened by sun and water within the soil—its potencies are unpredictable."[131]

CHAPTER 15

THE MOVE OUTWARD

THE EMERGENCE OF THE TEACHERS

The emergence of the teachers onto the world stage will be a group effort carried out over a number of years. The preparatory work for this event has been underway for some time now as individuals who form part of the Masters' groups have emerged and begun to institute changes in all fields of endeavor.

Many questions will naturally arise when we consider the externalization process. How will the teachers appear? Will they go through the long and slow process of human birth and development? Clearly we can't know the answers to these and the many other questions that naturally arise when we seriously consider this subject. But it is safe to assume that before these events can begin to unfold, serious changes will have to be implemented in our world that will result in a general easing of outer conditions. While it may appear that events of this magnitude would be impossible to realize in a world such as ours, it is helpful to keep in mind that there are powerful subjective forces at play that will aid and facilitate this process—forces that we cannot know or understand.

The wisdom teachings indicate that the timing for the actual emergence of the Masters will be decided in the year 2025. How rapidly or slowly the process unfolds after then is dependent upon humanity. We are told that three main requirements must be met before the World Teacher can appear. The first, and in many ways the most important requirement, is that the principle of sharing must begin to govern economic affairs. The second prerequisite is that the political and religious groups must begin to clean house. And finally, a measure of peace must be established in the world. None of these requirements is beyond humanity's ability to achieve, and much progress is being made along all three lines, but many hard decisions still remain to be ironed out.[132]

It must be reiterated that the teachers can only emerge as humanity prepares the way. The passivity inherent in the old paradigm of a returning savior who comes to end our suffering has no relationship to the facts and only contributes to the general condition of inertia that too often characterizes people who believe in these ideas. The new Aquarian perspective reverses the situation and posits the idea that the World Teacher can only appear *after humanity* has done its salvaging work.

There is another curious reversal of this whole process that is occurring at this time. Anyone who has studied the work of the Christ's disciples after his death will recognize that they were working under the inspiration of his energy field—they were, in effect, overshadowed. The energy from their teacher sustained and enabled them to bring his message to the world.

Today this process of overshadowing is occurring now, *before* the emergence of the teachers onto the physical plane. It is this overshadowing energy, emanating from the Masters and the World Teacher and conditioning the mental plane, that is enabling the people actively serving the Plan to undertake the difficult work they are doing and to withstand the enormous pressure of the forces that stand arrayed against them.[133]

In addition to this overshadowing on the mental plane there is also an overshadowing that is occurring on emotional levels, bringing hierarchical energy into the radius of many people. The love that emanates from the Hierarchy is being poured out onto the masses of humanity when they gather together for spiritual purposes.[134] This process of overshadowing is accustoming humanity to an ever-increasing rate of spiritual vibration.

Because of the nature of the work that they come to do, many of the most advanced members of the Hierarchy will not appear among us through the long and slow process of birth and development as is the case for average humanity. In some cases they will "appropriate" or overshadow the vehicles or bodies of individuals who have been prepared for this responsibility through an intense period of training. This work will resemble the experiment in overshadowing mentioned earlier that occurred with Krishnamurti. Some of the teachers will work through other individuals who willingly give over their bodies for use in the work that needs to be done. Individuals who cooperate in this way will necessarily be highly evolved and will consciously cooperate with the process that is occurring to them.

Other Masters will appear by manifesting a physical vehicle, called a *Mayavirupa*. This is a Sanskrit term for "the body of temporary manifestation which the Adept creates on occasion through the power of the will and in which He functions in order to make certain contacts on the physical plane and to engage in certain work for the race."[135] Other Masters will work through their present physical vehicles, which do not age or decline in health at the same rate as do normal human bodies. Having fully mastered the laws of supply and demand, the Masters are able to live many more years within the same body than is possible for humanity.

It is helpful to keep in mind that the Hierarchy is not coming forward solely to aid in the evolution of human consciousness but also to help carry forward certain developments within its own ranks. The Masters have their own life, goals, and destiny that differ quite naturally from the goals of ordinary human evolution. Humanity is just one link within the great chain that unites all forms of life within the bonds of light and love. The Plan that is working out on our planet, therefore, has for its keynote the great theme of *relationship* through which each kingdom contributes its part to the beautiful tapestry that together constitutes the outer raiment of the will of God.

At this time the Hierarchy is facing its own point of spiritual crisis in its evolutionary development. Its members stand before the door that leads to what is called the path of the Higher Evolution (seven cosmic paths of service from which they must choose), just as we stand before the door of initiation. The decisions confronting them are much more difficult than those we face. Both kingdoms, therefore, stand poised and ready to move forward. But the Hierarchy can only fulfill its destiny once the process of externalization has begun. There is a law that is working out at this time that requires the teachers' externalization into outer physical presence in order to realize their goal.

THE RETURN OF THE WORLD TEACHER

> It is the *Fire of Love* which He will bring; it is the message of the purificatory fire which He will sound.... He will impart the fire which burns and destroys all barriers in human nature, all separating walls between individuals, between groups and between nations. Are you prepared as individuals, as disciples and aspirants to submit yourselves to this fire?
>
> Alice Bailey, *Discipleship in the New Age, Vol. II,*

Finally, after the externalization of certain members of the Hierarchy, the World Teacher will appear among us in physical form. Some individuals today proclaim that the teacher, whom they call Maitreya, is already here and working behind the scenes through the transmission of channeled messages. However, the quality of this particular teaching and message reveals the fallacy of the claims and sadly distorts and discredits the whole intention and purpose of the teaching on the reappearance. The coming teacher will not spout platitudes through any spokesperson and does not need to be proclaimed as the awaited One by anyone. The Christ said, "By their works ye shall know them," and this will prove outstandingly to be the case in regard to this coming Teacher.

Of the reappearance the Tibetan wrote,

> The symbolic prophecies found in all the world Scriptures anent
> this imminent event will prove their veracity; their symbolism will
> nevertheless elicit reinterpretation, and circumstances and happen-
> ings will not necessarily be exactly as the Scriptures would appear to
> indicate. For instance, He will come indeed 'in the clouds of the air'
> as the Christian Scriptures say (Matt. XXIV.30), but of what great
> interest is that when millions come and go in the clouds each hour
> of the day and of the night? I mention this as one of the outstanding
> prophecies and one of the most familiar; it is, however, one which
> means little in our modern civilization. The fact that is of importance
> is that He will come.[136]

The World Teacher is the great Lord of Compassion. He is
sustained by the energy of cosmic love that pours through him.
Ever since he supposedly left us two thousand years ago, he has
stayed with us. He has lived in a physical body, dwelling in the
Himalayas, and works in close cooperation with the other teachers who also reside there. The Tibetan wrote of him: "Daily He
pours out His blessing on the world, and daily He stands under
the great pine in His garden at the sunset hour with hands uplifted
in blessing over all those who truly and earnestly seek to aspire."[137]
As people throughout the world link up with him and reach out to
touch his aura, a great quickening will occur, creating a powerful
chain reaction throughout the world.

His appearance at this dawning of the Aquarian Age will be
different than the work he undertook in Palestine two thousand
years ago when he overshadowed the Master Jesus. Today he will
appear as the supreme Head of the Spiritual Hierarchy, as the
"Water-Carrier," meeting the need of the people of the world.
People today are thirsty for truth, for right human relations and
for loving understanding, and he will satisfy that need.

He will choose to work among the group of individuals that
has done the most effective preparatory work. As stated earlier, it
is unlikely that He will emerge in the field of religion—it is much

more likely that He will work through the field of education or diplomacy, broadly defined. He could be French, South African, or Indian; we just don't know. What we do know is that when He emerges, He will found a "focal point," a type of heart center within the planet through which the love energy of the Hierarchy will ceaselessly flow.

For centuries, the people of the world have looked for the return of a World Teacher, but still He has not come. This book has attempted to show why this time is different from all other times within the long history of the planet in terms of its importance and opportunity. It is the time for which the spiritual Hierarchy has been preparing for 17.5 million years. St. Paul wrote, "The whole creation groaneth and travaileth together in pain until now, waiting for the manifestation of the Sons of God." The World Teacher, along with the Hierarchy, *wait*—having done all they can. It is now up to humanity to take the lead; everything now depends upon the right action of the men and women of goodwill.

We are asked to take heart in the recognition that the Hierarchy "stands," that the World Teacher is attentive to the voice of humanity, and that both are drawing closer each year to the time of return. The collective demand of humanity has gone forth to on high, the Teacher must respond, and "in such an hour as you think not, He *will come*." The timing of the coming flowering of events is not for us to know, but if our work is rightly done, the Teacher will come at the set and appointed time. How, where, or when He will come is not our concern. Our work is to do what we can, on as large a scale as possible, to bring about the right conditions—for His appearance depends upon that.

THE RELEASE OF THE ENERGY OF LOVE

In closing, may I beg all of you to go forward. Let nothing in the past—physical inertia, mental depression, lack of emotional control—keep you from taking fresh hold and with joy and interest making that needed progress which will fit you for more active and useful service. That none of you may be hindered by the past or by the present, but may live as Onlookers, is the prayer, constant and believing, of your teacher.

Alice Bailey, A Treatise on the Seven Rays, Vol. I

Humanity's heart is opening—beneath the outer coarseness and fragmentation a deep river of love is flowing strong. It is this love that will make all of the events that we have been discussing possible. But we have to be careful. During periods such as the present, the stimulation can be such that we will be tested and challenged in ways we might never have expected. It is, therefore, our duty to stand steady amidst these challenges.

We can see, for example, how opportunities were lost in the aftermath of key moments in our recent planetary history such as World War II, the 1960s, the fall of the Berlin Wall in 1989, and September 11, 2001. In the wake of each of these happenings there arose an almost immediate and powerful backlash by the conservative forces that served to block and deflect a measure of the inpouring light. We have to be wiser now so as to assure that we will not take precipitous action that could jeopardize or crush the promise of the opportunity of this moment. The issues at stake are too vital to the future of the planet as a whole.

The world's greatest revolutionary leader, the Christ, taught that the most powerful force in the world is love. It is love that enables us to sacrifice the part in the interests of the whole. We can learn the means to translate this love into a message that conditions and permeates all of our actions—not necessarily into an organization or any particular form, but rather into a revolutionary spirit that will prove powerful enough to change the world. Increasingly groups will emerge that are composed of people whose personalities are merged into one forward swing, whose rhythm is one and whose unity is so firmly established within the bonds of brotherhood that nothing can stop them. Through such groups the energy of the Hierarchy can work and the new world stand revealed.

It is said that nothing can stop an idea whose time has come. But sometimes it seems this is not true—sometimes it seems that many good ideas have indeed been stopped by the weight of inertia and the fears of the men and women of goodwill who have allowed their dreams and hopes to be squashed by the powerful forces that stand opposed to them.

A little vision can be a negative thing if it breeds a sense of futility or complacency. Sometimes the enormity of the task before us weakens our resolve. It is this passivity, and perhaps the pride in possessing special knowledge, that has fragmented the spiritual groups in the world—weakening the power that could flow from a united and mutually supportive effort.

Inertia is one of the principal conditions responsible for delaying the realization of the events that we have been discussing. And one of the primary aims of this book is to help awaken the sense of responsibility that is latent within us all but can be fanned into a bigger flame by the sharing of ideas such as these. If we come to recognize the true nature of what is currently happening upon our planet, how can we help but want to contribute in some way towards its realization? Perhaps we prefer to sit on the sidelines, observing. That's okay for a time; if we are educating ourselves, we need time to do that. But if we are serious and understand the implications of these ideas, our direction will surely change as we come to understand the wisdom of the teaching that states that "the disciple knows because he [or she] works" and not the other way around.

It is easy to compare ourselves to others and shrink back in the comparison. If we don't measure up, we feel we can leave the work to be done to those who do. But we can't afford to indulge in such thinking at this time. Let us fight these tendencies and unite around basic and powerful principles to bring about real change in our world. We are all needed, everyone has a part to play, and the more we align ourselves with hierarchical intent, the more rapidly our individual shortcomings will begin to take a back seat to our dedication to a higher and nobler cause.

Alice Bailey once commented that the Masters of the Wisdom must be quite desperate indeed if they had to work through such a flawed individual as she. To us she was a great worker, but she knew herself and her human limitations. It was her conclusion (based upon her own experience and observation) that many more people could move forward rapidly on the path and serve the Plan with greater resourcefulness if only they cared enough. The whole intent of her work with the Tibetan was to call upon people to awaken to the spiritual opportunity that is unfolding upon the planet, to move past their inertia and their shortcomings, their pride and their separatism, and demonstrate a willingness to play their part in cooperation with others for the greatest good of the greatest number. This book is dedicated to the new generation of seekers because it is they who will shape and transform the world and usher in the new age. They have been prepared to do this and the technology exists to make it possible.

The real error, the real death, is death as it exists in the form of a crystallized consciousness. All true seekers and men and women of goodwill take a stand against the death of liberty, the death of free speech, the death of freedom in human action, and the death of truth. These vital freedoms and their erosion in our world are what should concern us at this time; these are the fundamental principles that are now being systematically threatened and, if they continue to be negated, will prevent our entry into the new age. Men and women everywhere must work for the defeat of all forces that infringe upon human free will and seek to keep humanity in ignorance and darkness through the imposition of the lower will. The time is relatively short in which to achieve the goals that are set before us, and that is why we need to cultivate the spiritual will, for it is this will that can propel us past the inertia and clarify our priorities, moving us out of the ivory tower where we are all too often content to dwell and into the arena of constructive action.

In the midst of the present planetary crises we are stretched both vertically and horizontally, making it difficult at times to sense the new light that flows through the central point. But we work for the future. We may not live to experience the coming liberation in this one brief lifetime, but that doesn't matter, for we work for the larger whole, for the collective of those who come after us, which also includes the reincarnated aspects of ourselves.

The intention of this book has been to demonstrate that we can aid the incoming of the new day by preparing human minds and hearts for a deeper understanding of what is occurring at this time. The Tibetan has asked us to tell people everywhere that the Masters and their groups of disciples are actively working to bring order out of chaos. He has asked us to tell them that there IS a Plan, and that nothing can possibly arrest the working out of that Plan. People must be told that the Hierarchy and the World Teacher stand, and have stood for thousands of years, and are the expression of the accumulated wisdom of the ages. They must be told that above all else God is love, that the Hierarchy is love, and that the teacher is coming because he loves humanity.[138]

* * * * *

APPENDIX

SPIRITUAL PRACTICES

There are a number of simple practices, some of which have been mentioned in this book, which we can use to bring us into greater alignment with the worldwide group.

Group meditation at the time of the full and the new moons is particularly important. It serves to integrate us into the monthly cycle of the higher and lower interludes when the transformative energies are most potent. The keynotes for the different signs are as follows:

Aries: I come forth, and from the plane of mind I rule.

Taurus: I see, and when the eye is opened, all is illumined.

Gemini: I recognize my other self and in the waning of that self I grow and glow.

Cancer: I build a lighted house and therein dwell.

Leo: I am That and That am I.

Virgo: I am the Mother and the Child, I God, I matter am.

Libra: I choose the Way that leads between the two great lines of force.

Scorpio: Warrior I am, and from the battle I emerge triumphant.

Sagittarius: I see the goal. I reach the goal and see another.

Capricorn: Lost am I in light supernal and on that light I turn my back.

Aquarius: Water of life am I, poured forth for thirsty men.

Pisces: I leave the Father's home and turning back, I save.[139]

We can begin to participate in the "power points" of the daily cycle by using the following mantrams:

NOONTIME RECOLLECTION
I know O Lord of Life and Love about the need.
Touch my heart anew with love, that I, too, may love and give.

We can join with others around the world at 5:00 p.m. and use the Mantram of the New Group of World Servers.

May the Power of the One Life
pour through the group of all true servers.
May the Love of the One Soul,
characterize the lives of all who seek to aid the Great Ones.
May I fulfill my part in the One Work,
through self-forgetfulness, harmlessness and right speech.[140]

Each Thursday and Sunday are days for special group meditations. On Thursday the meditation is dedicated to the worldwide preparation for the Reappearance of the World Teacher:

REFLECTIVE MEDITATION UPON PREPARATION FOR THE REAPPEARANCE OF THE WORLD TEACHER

Stage I.

After achieving a positive and intended personality quietness, formulate clearly to yourself in your own words, the answers to the following questions:

1. As a member of the New Group of World Servers, what is my specific, fixed intention at this moment of dedicated contact with my soul?

2. Is my concentrated and expressed personality purpose in line with hierarchical intention—as far as I am permitted to know it?

3. Have I—in my own personal daily life—earned the right (because of definite effort and not so much because of success) to stand with those Servers Who are now undertaking the work of Preparation?

This is the one time in the meditation where you think of yourself, and it is here because it is a method of personality, focussed attention, and aligns your personality upon the mental plane.

Stage II.

Having answered these three questions in the light of the soul, then say with emphasis:

Forgetting the things which lie behind, I will strive towards my higher spiritual possibilities. I dedicate myself anew to the service of the Coming One and will do all I can to prepare humanity's mind and heart for that event. I have no other life intention.

PAUSE

Stage III.

1. Visualize the world situation as best you can and in terms of your major world interest and with what knowledge of world affairs you may possess. See the mass of men everywhere glowing with a dim light and, here and there, points of brighter light where members of the New Group of World Servers and men and women of spiritual intention and of loving hearts are working for humanity.

2. Then visualize (through the creative imagination) the vivid light of the Hierarchy, streaming towards humanity and slowly merging with the light which is already in men. Then say the first stanza of the Invocation:

> From the point of Light within the Mind of God
> Let Light stream forth into human minds.
> Let Light descend on Earth.

3. Then ponder upon the reappearance of the World Teacher and realize that no matter by what name He may be called in the many world religions, He is still the same great Identity; reflect and speculate upon the possible results of His appearance. Then say the second stanza of the Invocation:

> From the point of Love within the Heart of God
> Let Love stream forth into human hearts.
> May the Coming One return to Earth.

4. Endeavour to concentrate your fixed intention to serve and to spread love in your surroundings and realise that insofar as can do these things you are attempting to blend your personal will with the divine Will. Then say stanza three of the Invocation:

From the Centre where the Will of God is known
Let Purpose guide all little human wills—
The Purpose which the Masters know and serve.

5. Consider practically what you can do in the coming week to further the preparations for the coming of the World Teacher.

PAUSE

Then sound the OM three times, dedicating the threefold personality to the work of preparation.

Suggestions:

1. It is suggested that you do this meditation once every week, each Thursday, in the place of your usual meditation; endeavour to assume an attitude of aspiration, devotion, prayer and fixed intention (in this order), prior to following the outline. Esoteric students need the heart approach, as well as the mental approach, in order to make this meditation the powerful instrument which it can be.
2. Between Thursdays endeavor to carry out the results of the reflection expressed in this meditation. Lay practical plans and then review each week the planned activities when you sit down to this meditation, in the light of your expressed Intention.
3. Make this meditation brief and dynamic. After doing it a few times, this should be easily possible; forget the various stages and be impelled by the sequence and the synthesis of the form.[141]

* * * * *

On Sunday many people use the money meditation to help regenerate the money energy in the world:

REFLECTIVE MEDITATION ON ATTRACTING MONEY FOR HIERARCHICAL PURPOSES

Stage I.

After achieving a positive and intended personality quietness, formulate clearly to yourself and in your own words, the answers to the following questions:

1. If money is one of the most important things needed today for spiritual work, what is the factor which is at present deflecting it away from the work of the Hierarchy?
2. What is my personal attitude towards money? Do I regard it as a great and possible spiritual asset, or do I think of it in material terms?
3. What is my personal responsibility in regard to money which passes through my hands? Am I handling it as a disciple of the Masters should handle it?

PAUSE

Stage II.

1. Ponder on the redemption of humanity through the right use of money. Visualise the money in the world today as

   a. Concretized energy, at present largely used for purely material purposes and for the satisfaction (where the individual is concerned) of purely personal desires.

   b. Visualize money as a great stream of flowing golden substance, passing out of the control of the Forces of Materialism into the control of the Forces of Light.

2. Then say the following invocative prayer, with focused mental concentration and from a heartfelt desire to meet spiritual demands:

O Thou in Whom we live and move and have our being, the Power that can make all things new, turn to spiritual purposes the money in the world; touch the hearts of men everywhere so that they may give to the work of the Hierarchy that which has hitherto been given to material satisfaction. The New Group of World Servers needs money in large quantities. I ask that the needed vast sums may be made available. May this potent energy of Thine be in the hands of the Forces of Light.

3. Then visualize the work to be done by those groups which claim your present allegiance (i.e., the Arcane School and the Service Activities, or any other group which you know is attempting to carry out the hierarchical Plan). Then, through the creative imagination and by an act of the will, see untold and unlimited sums of money pouring into the hands of those who seek to do the Masters' work.

4. Then say aloud, with conviction and emphasis:

He for Whom the whole world waits has said that whatsoever shall be asked in His Name and with faith in the response will see it accomplished.

Remember at the same time that "faith is the substance of things hoped for and the evidence of things not seen." Then add:

I ask for the needed money for . . . . and can demand it because

From the Center which we call the human race
Let the Plan of Love and Light work out.
And may it seal the door where evil dwells.

5. Close with a careful consideration of your own responsibility to the Plan, and each week plan your financial cooperation with the Hierarchy. Be practical and realistic and know that if you do not give, you may not ask, for you have no right to evoke that which you do not share.

Suggestions:

1. This meditation is so simple that many of you may regard it as innocuous and perhaps futile. Used by many simultaneously, it may shatter the impasse which at present prevents adequate funds pouring into the work which the Hierarchy seeks to accomplish.
2. Do this meditation every Sunday morning. Take what you have saved during the previous week and dedicate it to the work and present it in meditation to the Christ and His Hierarchy. Whether the sum is large or small, it can become an attractive and magnetic unit in the Masters' plans.
3. Realize the Law that "to those who give shall be given" so that they can give again.
4. Attempt to feel true love sweeping through you, and have the fixed intention to express this love to all you contact. It is the great attractive and selfless agent in world affairs.[142]

These two meditations, perhaps more than all others, serve the purposes of the Plan for our planet which is, pre-eminently, the work of preparation for the advent of the World Teacher.

The four stanzas of the Great Invocation are used in these two meditations but, curiously, its last line is omitted. Surely there must be a reason for this, especially since in many ways the last line powerfully encapsulates the intention of the Invocation as a whole. Perhaps it is this simple, direct, and powerful line, "Let Light and Love and Power restore the Plan on Earth," which could, in and of itself, serve as a mantric tool for distribution. In this day of sound bites and fractured attention spans, perhaps this one line might be able to make a foothold into human consciousness and spark peoples' curiosity and lead them later to the use of the Great Invocation in its entirety.

In addition to the above suggestions there are special mantrams and esoteric phrases that we can use at any time of the day and that will serve to align us with the group objectives of service.

ANCIENT MANTRAM

Lead us, O Lord,
from darkness to light;
from the unreal to the real;
from death to immortality.
(Brihadaranyaki Upanishad I, 3, 28)[143]

GAYATRI

O Thou Who givest sustenance to the Universe
From Whom all things proceed
To Whom all things return,
Unveil to us the face of the true spiritual sun
Hidden by a disk of golden light.
That we may know the truth and do our whole duty
As we journey to Thy sacred feet.[144]

This ancient prayer can used effectively at the sunset hour.

AFFIRMATION OF THE DISCIPLE

I am a point of light within a greater Light.
I am a strand of loving energy within
the stream of love divine.

I am a point of sacrificial Fire,
focussed within the fiery Will of God.
And thus I stand.

I am a way by which men may achieve.
I am a source of strength, enabling them to stand.
I am a beam of light, shining upon their way.
And thus I stand.

And standing thus revolve
And tread this way the ways of men,
And know the ways of God.
And thus I stand.

This mantram embodies the attitude of the disciple who is striving to serve in alignment with his or her soul. The Tibetan wrote of this mantram, "There is a certain esoteric Mantram which embodies this attitude—the attitude of the disciple who is striving, in cooperative endeavour with others, to link hierarchical intent with human aspiration and thus bring humanity nearer to its goal."[145]

MANTRAM OF UNIFICATION

The sons of men are one and I am one with them.
I seek to love, not hate;
I seek to serve and not exact due service;
I seek to heal, not hurt.

Let pain bring due reward of light and love.
Let the soul control the outer form, and life
and all events,
And bring to light the love
that underlies the happenings of the time.

Let vision come and insight.
Let the future stand revealed.
Let inner union demonstrate and
outer cleavages be gone.
Let love prevail.
Let all men love.[146]

Every morning, at noon, and each night before retiring to sleep, align yourself with your soul, with the Ashram and with me, and say very quietly and with no tension:

I stand a point of peace,
and through the point which I can thus provide,
love and true light can flow.

I stand in restful poise, and through that poise
I can attract the gifts which I must give—
an understanding heart, a quiet mind—myself.

I never am alone, for round me gather
those I seek to serve,
my brothers in the Ashram, souls that demand my help,
e'en though I see them not, and those in distant places
who seek the Master of my life,
my brother, the Tibetan.[147]

THE RULES OF THE ROAD

1. The Road is trodden in the full light of day, thrown upon the Path by Those Who know and lead. Naught can then be hidden, and at each turn upon that Road a man must face himself.
2. Upon the Road the hidden stands revealed. Each sees and knows the villainy of each. And yet there is, with that great

revelation, no turning back, no spurning of each other, no shakiness upon the Road. The Road goes forward into day.

3. Upon that Road one wanders not alone. There is no rush, no hurry. And yet there is no time to lose. Each pilgrim, knowing this, presses his footsteps forward, and finds himself surrounded by his fellowmen. Some move ahead; he follows after. Some move behind; he sets the pace. He travels not alone.

4. Three things the Pilgrim must avoid. The wearing of a hood, a veil which hides his face from others; the carrying of a water pot which only holds enough for his own wants; the shouldering of a staff without a crook to hold.

5. Each Pilgrim on the Road must carry with him what he needs: a pot of fire, to warm his fellowmen; a lamp, to cast its rays upon his heart and show his fellowmen the nature of his hidden life; a purse of gold, which he scatters not upon the Road, but shares with others; a sealed vase, wherein he carries all his aspiration to cast before the feet of Him Who waits to greet him at the gate—a sealed vase.

6. The Pilgrim, as he walks upon the Road, must have the open ear, the giving hand, the silent tongue, the chastened heart, the golden voice, the rapid foot, and the open eye which sees the light. He knows he travels not alone.[148]

Introductory meditative training and a study guide
are available from the Seven Ray Institute,
www.sevenray.org.

NOTES

[1] Alice Bailey, *Esoteric Psychology, Vol. II,* pp. 217-18

[2] "Extract from a Statement by the Tibetan" August 1934

[3] Alice Bailey, *The Reappearance of the Christ,* Lucis Publishing Company, 1948, p. 80

[4] *Ibid.,* p. 81

[5] Alice Bailey, *Discipleship in the New Age, Vol. II,* 1955, p. 48

[6] Alice Bailey, *The Reappearance of the Christ,* p. 52-53

[7] *Ibid*

[8] Alice Bailey, *Glamour: A World Problem,* p. 96. *The Old Commentary* describes the etheric body as the "reality which shines under the envelope which envelops it."

[9] Alice Bailey, *The Rays and the Initiations,* 1960, p. 716

[10] Alice Bailey, *The Externalisation of the Hierarchy,* 1957, p. 536

[11] Alice Bailey, *The Reappearance of the Christ,* p. 69

[12] Alice Bailey, *A Treatise on White Magic,* 1951, pp. 426–27

[13] Alice Bailey, *The Reappearance of the Christ,* p. 8

[14] Alice Bailey, *The Externalisation of the Hierarchy,* p. 612

[15] *Ibid.,* p. 652

[16] Alice Bailey, *The Reappearance of the Christ,* p. 125

[17] Alice Bailey, *The Externalisation of the Hierarchy,* p. 612

[18] Encyclopedic Theosophical Glossary, 1999 by Theosophical University Press

[19] Alice Bailey, *The Externalisation of the Hierarchy.,* p. 686–87

[20] Alice Bailey, *Esoteric Psychology, Vol. I,* 1962, p. 293

[21] In Tibetan Buddhism, Tara is known as the "Mother of the Buddhas," she who hears the cries of the world.

[22] Alice Bailey, *A Treatise on White Magic*, p. 378

[23] *Ibid.*, p. 379

[24] Alice Bailey, *Discipleship in the New Age, Vol. II*, p. 409

[25] Alice Bailey, *Esoteric Healing*, 1953, p. 231

[26] Alice Bailey, *Initiation, Human and Solar*, 1951, p. 35

[27] Alice Bailey, *The Rays and the Initiations*, p. 554

[28] Alice Bailey, *Discipleship in the New Age, Vol. II*, p. 166

[29] Alice Bailey, *Ibid.*, pp. 171–72

[30] Alice Bailey, *The Rays and the Initiations*, p. 212

[31] Alice Bailey, *The Unfinished Autobiography*, 1951, pp. 35–36

[32] *Ibid.*, pp. 162–63

[33] *Ibid.*, p. 164

[34] *Ibid.*, p. 299

[35] Alice Bailey, *The Rays and the Initiations*, p. 255

[36] Alice Bailey, *Esoteric Psychology, Vol. I*, p. 300

[37] Alice Bailey, *A Treatise on White Magic*, p. 203

[38] Alice Bailey, *Esoteric Psychology, Vol. II*, p. 210

[39] Alice Bailey, *The Destiny of the Nations*, 1949, p. 45

[40] Alice Bailey, *Esoteric Healing*, p. 319

[41] *Ibid.*, p. 230

[42] Alice Bailey, *A Treatise on White Magic*, pp. 499–500

[43] Alice Bailey, *Ibid*, p. 505

[44] Alice Bailey, *The Destiny of the Nations*, p. 3-4

[45] *Ibid.*, p. 145

[46] Alice Bailey, *Discipleship in the New Age, Vol. I*, 1944, pp. 315, 350

[47] Alice Bailey, *A Treatise on White Magic*, p. 112

[48] Alice Bailey, *The Destiny of the Nations*, p. 39

[49] Alice Bailey, *Discipleship in the New Age, Vol. I*, p. 38

[50] Alice Bailey, *Esoteric Psychology, Vol. I*, p. 207

[51] *Ibid.*, p. 209

[52] Alice Bailey, *A Treatise on Esoteric Astrology*, 1951, p. 5

[53] Alice Bailey, *Discipleship in the New Age, Vol. I*, pp. 583–84

[54] Alice Bailey, *The Rays and the Initiations.*, p. 352

[55] Alice Bailey, *Glamour: A World Problem*, 1953, pp. 69–70

[56] Alice Bailey, *Esoteric Psychology, Vol. I*, pp. 201-210

[57] Alice Bailey, *Esoteric Psychology, Vol. II*, p. 155

[58] Alice Bailey, *Letters on Occult Meditation, 1950*, p. 338-39

[59] Alice Bailey, *Discipleship in the New Age, Vol. I*, p. 95

[60] Alice Bailey, *Ibid*, p. 77

[61] Alice Bailey, *Glamour: A World Problem*, p. 45

[62] Alice Bailey, *Destiny of the Nations*, p. 29

[63] See *Destiny of the Nations*

[64] Alice Bailey, *Destiny of the Nations*, p. 29

[65] Alice Bailey, *Discipleship in the New Age, Vol. II*, pp. 425-26

[66] Alice Bailey, *Destiny of the Nations*, p. 33

[67] Alice Bailey, *Discipleship in the New Age, Vol. I*, p. 6

[68] Alice Bailey, *The Externalisation of the Hierarchy*, p. 335

[69] Alice Bailey, *Esoteric Astrology*, p. 235

[70] Alice Bailey, *Esoteric Psychology, Vol. I*, p. 306

[71] Alice Bailey, *Ibid*, pp. 306–07

[72] Alice Bailey, *Ibid*, p. 298–299

[73] Alice Bailey, *A Treatise on White Magic*, p. 132

[74] Alice Bailey, *The Rays and the Initiations*, p. 286

[75] Alice Bailey, *A Treatise on Cosmic Fire*, p. 909

[76] Alice Bailey, *The Rays and the Initiations*, p. 552

[77] Alice Bailey, *Esoteric Psychology, Vol. I*, p. 26

[78] Alice Bailey, *The Light of the Soul*, 1955, p. xv

[79] *Bhagavad Gita*, VI, 16–17

[80] Alice Bailey, *Discipleship in the New Age, Vol. II*, p. 768

[81] Alice Bailey, *Glamour, A World Problem*, 1950, p. 232

[82] Alice Bailey, *Esoteric Psychology, Vol. II*, 1942, p. 122

[83] Alice Bailey, *Esoteric Psychology, Vol. II*, pp. 128–29

[84] Alice Bailey, *Discipleship in the New Age, Vol. I*, p. 726

[85] Alice Bailey, *The Reappearance of the Christ*, pp. 166–171

[86] Alice Bailey, *Esoteric Psychology, Vol. II*, p. 132

[87] Alice Bailey, *A Treatise on White Magic*, pp. 319–21

[88] Alice Bailey, *The Rays and the Initiations*, p. 95

[89] Alice Bailey, *Discipleship in the New Age, Vol. II*, p. 168

[90] Alice Bailey, *Discipleship in the New Age, Vol. II*, p. 157

[91] Alice Bailey, *The Rays and the Initiations*, p. 759

[92] *Ibid.*, p. 250-51

[93] Alice Bailey, See *A Treatise on Cosmic Fire*, 1951, p. 93 and *Esoteric Astrology*, p. 13

[94] Alice Bailey, *Esoteric Psychology, Vol. II*, pp. 686–87

[95] Alice Bailey, *Discipleship in the New Age, Vol. I*, p. 642

[96] Alice Bailey, *Esoteric Psychology, Vol. II*, p. 693

[97] Extracted from a booklet, "The Wesak Festival," offered by the Lucis Trust

[98] Alice Bailey, *Discipleship in the New Age, Vol. I*, p. 629

[99] Alice Bailey, *The Externalisation of the Hierarchy*, p. 25

[100] *Ibid.*, p. 352

[101] Alice Bailey, *The Rays and the Initiations*, p. 88

[102] Alice Bailey, *The Externalisation of the Hierarchy*, p. 480

[103] Alice Bailey, *The Rays and the Initiations*, p. 760

[104] Alice Bailey, *The Externalisation of the Hierarchy*, pp. 226–27

[105] Alice Bailey, *A Treatise on White Magic*, p. 194

[106] Alice Bailey, *Esoteric Psychology, Vol. II*, p. 539

[107] Alice Bailey, *Initiation, Human and Solar*, p. 198

[108] Alice Bailey, *Discipleship in the New Age, Vol. I*, p. 644

[109] Alice Bailey, *The Externalisation of the Hierarchy*, p. 516

[110] See *Esoteric Healing* pages 103-05

[111] Alice Bailey, *A Treatise on White Magic*, p. 182

[112] Alice Bailey, *Discipleship in the New Age, Vol. II*, p. 172

[113] Alice Bailey, *Discipleship in the New Age, Vol. I*, p. 77-78

[114] Alice Bailey, *Letters on Occult Meditation*, pp. 268–69

[115] Alice Bailey, *The Rays and the Initiations*, p. 4

[116] Alice Bailey, *The Reappearance of the Christ*, p. 86

[117] Alice Bailey, *Esoteric Psychology, Vol. I*, p. xviii

[118] Alice Bailey, *The Rays and the Initiations.*, p. 569

[119] Alice Bailey, *A Treatise on White Magic*, p. 62

[120] Alice Bailey, *The Rays and the Initiations*, p. 674

[121] Alice Bailey, *Discipleship in the New Age, Vol. I*, pp. 538–39

[122] *Ibid.*, p. 691

[123] *Ibid.*, pp. 115–16

[124] *Ibid.*, p. 695

[125] *Ibid.*, p. 704

[126] *Ibid.*, p. 123

[127] H.P. Blavatsky, *Studies in Occultism*, Theosophical University Press.

[128] Mary Bailey was the third President of the Lucis Trust and second wife of Foster Bailey.

[129] Alice Bailey, *The Rays and the Initiations*, p. 213

[130] Alice Bailey, *Discipleship in the New Age, Vol. II*, p. 225-27

[131] Alice Bailey, *The Externalisation of the Hierarchy*, pp. 27-28

[132] Alice Bailey, *The Externalisation of the Hierarchy*, p. 616

[133] Alice Bailey, *The Rays and the Initiations*, p. 615

[134] *Ibid.*

[135] *Ibid.*, p. 697; see also *A Treatise on Cosmic Fire*, footnote, p. 761

[136] Alice Bailey, *The Reappearance of the Christ.*, p. 45

[137] Alice Bailey, *Initiation, Human and Solar*, p. 44

[138] *Ibid*, p. 701

[139] Alice Bailey, *Esoteric Astrology*, p. 653-54

[140] Alice Bailey, *A Treatise on White Magic*, p. 261

[141] Alice Bailey, *Discipleship in the New Age, Vol. II*, pp. 226-28

[142] *Ibid.*, pp. 228-31

[143] Alice Bailey, *Glamour: A World Problem*, p. 198

[144] Alice Bailey, *The Rays and the Initiations*, p. 756

[145] Alice Bailey, *Telepathy and the Etheric Vehicle*, p. 197

[146] Alice Bailey, *Discipleship in the New Age, Vol. I*, p. 790

[147] Alice Bailey, *Discipleship in the New Age, Vol. II*, pp. 723-24

[148] Alice Bailey, *Discipleship in the New Age, Vol. I.*, pp. 583-84

Suggested Reading List and Esoteric Groups

AGNI YOGA
Agni Yoga
AUM
Brotherhood
Infinity I, II
Hierarchy
Heart
Fiery World I, II, & III
Leaves of Morya's Garden I, II
New Era Community
Supermundane I, II, III, & IV

ARMSTRONG, Karen
The Battle for God
Buddha
A History of God
Muhammad: A Prophet for Our Time
Visions of God

AVALON, Arthur
The Serpent Power

BAILEY, Alice
The Consciousness of the Atom
The Destiny of the Nations
Discipleship in the New Age, Vols. I & II

The Externalisation of the Hierarchy
From Bethlehem to Calvary
From Intellect to Intuition
Glamour: A World Problem
Initiation, Human & Solar
Letters on Occult Meditation
The Labours of Hercules
The Light of the Soul
The Reappearance of the Christ
The Soul and its Mechanism
Telepathy and the Etheric Vehicle
A Treatise on Cosmic Fire
A Treatise on the Seven Rays:
    Vol. I, Esoteric Psychology
    Vol. II, Esoteric Psychology
    Vol. III Esoteric Astrology
    Vol. IV Esoteric Healing
    Vol. V The Rays and the Initiations
A Treatise on White Magic
The Unfinished Autobiography

COMPILATIONS FROM THE ABOVE TEXTS
Animal Kingdom: A Spiritual Perspective
A Compilation on Sex
Death: the Great Adventure
Ponder on This
Serving Humanity
The Seventh Ray: Revealer of the New Age

BAILEY, Foster
   Reflections
   The Spirit of Masonry

BAILEY, Mary
   A Learning Experience

BESANT, Annie
   Avataras
   Occult Chemistry
   A Study in Consciousness

BLAVATSKY, Helena P.
Isis Unveiled
The Secret Doctrine
The Theosophical Glossary
The Voice of the Silence

COLLINS, Mabel
Light on the Path

COSGROVE, Eugene
The High Walk of Discipleship
Letter to a Disciple
The Science of the Initiates

GOVINDA, Lama
Buddhist Reflections
The Way of the White Clouds

HEINDEL, Max
Rosicrucian Cosmo-Conception

HUMPRHEYS, Christmas
Buddhism
Studies in the Middle Way

JOHNSTON, Mr. Charles
The Bhagavad Gita
The Yoga Sutras of Patanjali

LINDSAY, Phillip
Destiny of the Races and Nations
The Hidden History of Humanity
Soul Cycles of the Seven Rays

NASH, Mr. John
Quest for the Soul
The Soul and Its Destiny

NIHLEN, Niklas
Islands of Celestial Waters
Also see <u>CosmoCycles1</u> (a Yahoo group)

ROERICH, Helena
Foundations of Buddhism
Letters of Helena Roerich, Vols. I & II

ROBBINS, Michael
The Tapestry of the Gods, Vol 1 & 2
www.makara.us

SCOTT, Mr. Cyril
The Greater Awareness
The Initiate
Music, Its Secret Influence Throughout the Ages

WOOD, Ernest
Concentration; An Approach to Meditation
The Seven Rays

YOGANANDA, Paramahansa
The Autobiography of a Yogi

YUKTESWAR, Sri
The Holy Science

ESOTERIC GROUPS

Agni Yoga Society, 319 West 107th Street, New York, NY 10025-2799
phone (212) 864-7752 • fax (212) 864-7704
e-mail: info@agniyoga.org, www.agniyoga,org

Aquarian Age Community,
233 Bay Street No. 206, Jersey City, NJ 07302
e-mail: commune@aquaac.org, http://www.aquaac.org/

Arkana Workshops,
3916 Sepulveda Boulevard Suite 107, Culver City, CA 90230
http://www.meditationtraining.org/

AstroNova, e-mail: astronova@comhem.se, www.astronova.nu

Blavatsky Net, www.blavatsky.net

The Centre for Esoteric Studies
  Lawrence Square, 700 Lawrence Ave. West, Suite 440
  Toronto, Ontario, Canada
  phone (416)929.5287, (519)599.5470
  www.centreesotericstudies.com

CosmoCycles1, (a Yahoo Group)

Eastern Tradition Research Institute, www.easterntradition.org

Esoteric Astrologer, www.esotericastrologer.org

Esoteric Quarterly, www.esotericstudies.net/quarterly

Fellowship of Cosmic Fire, (a Yahoo Group)

Golden Sufi Center, P.O. Box 428, Inverness, CA 94937-0428
  phone (415) 663-8773
  www.goldensufi.org

Grand Lodge Ancient Universal Mysteries
  P.O. Box 735, Planetarium Station, New York, NY 10024-0539
  www.grandlodgeaum.org

Internet Arcano, www.internetarcano.org

The Lifebridge Foundation, PO Box 327, High Falls, NY 12440
  phone (845)338-6418
  www.lifebridge.org

Lucis Trust
  also: Arcane School, Triangles, World Goodwill,
               Lucis Publishing Company
  120 Wall St., 24th Floor, New York, NY 10005
  www.lucistrust.org,

www.makara.us

Meditation Mount, PO Box 566, Ojai, CA USA 93024-0566
    phone (805)646-5508
    www.meditation.com

Path of Light, PO Box 804, Ashland, OR 97520
    phone (541)488-1322
    www.pathoflight.com

Pathways to Peace, www.pathways-to-peace.com

School of Ageless Wisdom,
    6005 Royaloak Dr, Arlington TX 76106-1035
    phone (817)654-1018
    rmswcc@airmail.net

School for Esoteric Studies
    275 S French Broad Ave, Asheville, NC 28801
    www.esotericstudies.net

Seven Ray Institute / University of the Seven Rays
    128 Manhattan Ave, Jersey City, NJ 07307-3812
    phone (201)798-7777
    sevenray@sevenray.com, www.sevenray.org

Seven Ray Forum, www.sevenray.net/sri_forum

Sufi Order International,
    North American Secretariat,
    5 Abode Rd, New Lebanon, NY 12125
    Mail to: PO Box 480
    phone (518)794-7834 (SUFI)
    www.sufiorder.org

Uriel, www.uriel.com

World Service Intergroup, www.synthesis.tc

About the Author

Kathy Newburn, a long-time student of the Ageless Wisdom teachings, worked for many years at the Lucis Trust, New York in various capacities. She presently works for the Seven Ray Institute and is affiliated with a number of spiritual groups in the New York area. Her work is focused upon helping to bring the Ageless Wisdom teachings to the new generation of seekers. She is the editor of *The Journal of Esoteric Psychology* and on the editorial board of *The Esoteric Quarterly*.

14479477R00112

Printed in Poland
by Amazon Fulfillment
Poland Sp. z o.o., Wrocław